Cloth for the Cradle

Cloth for the Cradle

Worship resources and readings for Advent, Christmas and Epiphany

The Wild Goose Worship Group

First published 1997

ISBN 1 901557 01 4

Copyright © 1997, Wild Goose Resource Group

Front cover: Graham Maule © 1997 Wild Goose Resource Group

The members of the Wild Goose Worship Group and of the
Wild Goose Resource Group have asserted their rights
under the Copyright, Designs and Patents Act, 1988,
to be identified as the authors of this work.

Published by Wild Goose Publications

Wild Goose Publications, Unit 15, Six Harmony Row, Glasgow G51 3BA

Wild Goose Publications is the publishing division of the Iona Community.
Scottish Charity No. SC003794. Limited Company Reg. No SCO96243.

The Wild Goose is the Celtic symbol of the Holy Spirit.
It is the trademark of Wild Goose Publications.

Distributed in Australia and New Zealand by Willow Connection Pty Ltd,
Unit 7A, 3-9 Kenneth Road, Manly Vale NSW 2093.

Permission to reproduce any part of this work in Australia or New Zealand
should be sought from Willow Connection.

A catalogue record for this book is available from the British Library.

Printed by The Cromwell Press Ltd, Melksham, Wilts.

To the people of Carnwadric,
to whom this book is fondly dedicated,
we express our profound gratitude.

Contents

Introduction

This is a book of bits.

You will not find here a complete liturgy or order of service. Nor will you find prayers or collects for all the Sundays in Advent. Nor will you find a complete nativity play. Nor will you find lots of things that children can do.

What you will find are bits, fragments, resources for shaping the worship of God's people during the seasons of Advent, Christmas and Epiphany.

This is the way the book has evolved because this is the way the Wild Goose Worship Group works – as enablers of what might be rather than as authors of what cannot be repeated.

The material contained here has been in circulation for between one and twelve years. Everything has been through our mouths and the mouths of other people and amended according to experience or suggestions. While none of the prayers or liturgical responses have been published before, some of the scripts have. But all have been revised, and (for the benefit of a wider public) pruned of most colloquialisms or translated from the original Scots. This should prevent vicars in Burnley phoning up to ask if Joseph must have a Glasgow accent.

While much of the material evolved for use in our own group worship, or for church services we were asked to lead, some developed through commitment to a local congregational setting.

For two years, two members of the group were associated with Carnwadric Parish Church in Glasgow where they met on most Thursday evenings to discover how worship in an urban priority area might be shaped and led by local people. That engagement turned on its head all college teaching about liturgy and all presumptions that the clergy knew best. Particularly in preparation for an Advent play which the adults would perform while the children watched, we realized how a purely academic approach to Scripture and to worship touches only a small percentage of God's people, and fails to involve those for whom intuition, experience and symbols are the means by which truth is discovered, embraced and celebrated.

To the people of Carnwadric, to whom this book is fondly dedicated, we express our profound gratitude.

Christmas is often referred to as 'a time for the children'. While no-one would deny the right of children to celebrate Jesus' birth, we have to guard against the season becoming a baby festival of maudlin sentimentality.

Those who witnessed and were involved in or around the Incarnation were all adults. Only Christ was small. Christmas therefore requires the adult world not to gaze on children re-enacting the Nativity, but rather to re-discover the stories of Christ's birth as speaking from and to adult experience.

There are plenty of nativity plays for those who can barely speak, let alone act. There is a dearth of material for those who have long since left their childhood, but who need to discover that Advent, Christmas and Epiphany belong to their present and not their earlier years.

It is hoped that this book of bits may well help to supply that need.

John L. Bell
for The Wild Goose Worship Group

Using this book

There are six basic types of material in the book, each of which is indicated by a recurrent symbol

△ **Liturgical Material**, often sets of shared responses for use of a leader and congregation.

○ **Prayers** which may be read by one person, with the occasional option of a congregational spoken or sung response.

| **Readings** which may be poems or monologues, normally requiring one reader.

∨ **Meditations** which will normally require one or more voices and may be accompanied by action.

☐ **Scripts** which may be read by two or more people and which may lend themselves to dramatic presentation.

↑ **Symbolic Actions** which enable the congregation to be actively engaged in the worship by physically moving around the building.

The material is arranged chronologically, roughly complementing the progress of the readings for the seasons. This, however, does not mean that a set of responses for Advent would be inappropriate in Epiphany. There is room for interchange.

It is envisaged that worship leaders will select materials from the book and incorporate them into acts of worship rather than make a liturgy simply out of what is found here. Or it may be that leaders will see in some of these resources, models which they might use to help devise their own materials.

However, a word might be offered with respect to the different types of material found here.

Liturgical material is, by and large, meant to be shared by the whole congregation. Therefore these items should be printed or photocopied onto service sheets.

We strongly advise people to use the same set of responses throughout the season of Advent, changing them when Christmas and then Epiphany come along. It is tedious to congregations to be asked to repeat a different set of words every Sunday.

Whether the responses are used at the beginning or end of worship, or precede or follow scripture readings is at the user's discretion.

Prayers need not be seen by everyone. They are meant to be read in the hearing of the congregation. They should therefore be rehearsed aloud in advance of worship, so that all the words feel comfortable in the reader's mouth. To give someone a prayer at the last minute or to glance at the prayer the minute before you read it, is insulting to God to whom the worship is offered and also to God's people on behalf of whom the prayer is said. Use of silence and sung or spoken congregational responses is encouraged where appropriate.

Readings may be suitable for some folk and not for others. As with prayers, adequate rehearsal is required both in private and in the space where the reading will be delivered.

The best readers are not those with contrived accents or drama school diplomas, but people who are prepared to be for the moment, the mouth of God (when reading Scripture) or the representative of one of God's biblical people (when reading a monologue). If the story or the poem or the words have gone through an individual's system several times, they will come out with conviction. If they have not done the rounds of his or her body, they will remain on the page.

While readings usually will be delivered facing a congregation, **Meditations** need not happen in the same way. It has been our experience, that people can engage imaginatively with meditative readings when they do not face the reader, but rather when the voice or voices come from the side or the back as appropriate.

The feeling of voices coming from around cannot happen when microphones and amplifiers are used. These channel all sound through the speakers, irrespective of where the reader is standing. A natural acoustic is therefore preferable and most buildings can be so used, if the congregation or audience sit together towards the front and if readers speak with their backs to a solid wall which becomes a sounding board.

Of course, the 'T-position' lobby will remind us that there are hard of hearing people in church. There are also people with limited mobility who cannot take part in every symbolic action. There are people with restricted vision who cannot see what is happening at the front. There are single people or couples without children who get annoyed by Christmas always being referred to as a 'family' time. And there are women who have lost babies during pregnancy or at birth, for whom the concentration on Mary's confinement causes them pain.

Those who lobby for people with one disadvantage cannot rule or amend everything that happens in worship. To allow for a minimal degree of temporary discomfort is to demonstrate that kind of hospitality to others which is central to the Christian faith.

Scripts, like readings, do not require gifted performers. Many of the dialogues included here can simply be read by people standing in appropriate parts of the worship space which will not inevitably be at the front of, but may be in the midst of or round the periphery of, the seated congregation.

For people who are keen to provide some kind of continuous narrative on the Nativity, there are a number of monologues and dialogues which may be used almost as an alternative to the classic 'Seven Lessons', in which case they should be complemented by songs which are alternatives to the classic 'Seven Carols'.

In the case of MICHAEL MOUSE P.102, it is preferable that this script be enacted, with characters of all ages dressed appropriately and with all words memorized.

Symbolic Actions should, in the main, be optional rather than obligatory. Not everyone feels easy about lighting a candle, or moving from their seat to a distant part of the church. This should be respected. Such people are often quite happy for others to engage in such action as long as they are not personally compelled.

When symbolic action is taking place, it is essential that all can see it. To assemble the crib as in CLOTH FOR THE CRADLE P.74, in such a position that only the front row will know what is going on, is to alienate the majority of the congregation. Similarly if the action in HOW FAR IS IT P.64, required four booths marked according to the main points of the compass, the signs for North, South, East and West etc. should not be six inches high and hung just above waist level. They should be big enough and hung high enough for all to see.

Just as we would like to encourage those who have purchased this book for its liturgical material to consider using some meditations or scripts, so we would encourage those who favour the latter also to try the former. There are too many false presumptions made about congregations by those who claim to 'know what they can take'. It has consistently surprised us to see high church Anglo Catholics, who seem thirled to the Prayer Book, relaxing when a humorous dialogue is employed sensitively and in the right place, just as it has amused us to see diehard orange Protestants warm at the prospect of doing the 'papish' thing of lighting a candle.

Finally, we encourage users of this material to think about the space in which it is used. Up to a third of the difficulties people encounter in trying something new in worship has to do with the building in which they meet, yet architecture and seating is often last on our list of things to be considered.

When people sit far apart, not only will they find it difficult to sing, they will find it awkward to laugh and difficult to listen. There is something enabling about being part *of* a congregation as distinct from being apart *from* the congregation. Of course, there is a place for personal piety, but the corporate worship of God's people should not always be held ransom to the needs of individuals to have their own sacred space. Jesus advised such folk to use their closet.

Because most lay people do not spend their time prancing about chancels or speaking from lecterns, the more comfortable leaders can feel, in moving around the building or hearing their voice sound in it, the better.

There are lots of other things we would like to say, but too many words of advice might be more of a hindrance than a help.

We therefore encourage you to enjoy using the material in the book.

Reproducing the material

Unless indicated otherwise, the material in CLOTH FOR THE CRADLE is copyright © Wild Goose Resource Group.

Permission to reproduce the material for one-off, *non-commercial* purposes (in local worship or educational settings) is granted, free of charge, with the purchase of the book. In these cases, the copyright source should be clearly indicated, as follows:

copyright © 1997 WGRG, Iona Community, Glasgow G51 3UU, Scotland.

If wishing to reproduce any of the material for *commercial* purposes (eg. inclusion in a book or recording for sale, or workshop material for which a fee is to be charged) permission must be sought in writing from the Wild Goose Resource Group at the above address.

Advent
Resources

△ Behind the corridors of space
Advent responses 1

Leader: Behind the corridors of space,
before the world began,
beyond all understanding . . .
God.

Words and music traditional

Glo-ri-a, Glo-ri-a, Glo-ri-a, in ex-cel-sis De - o.

Fathering time,
mothering creation,
parenting all people . . .
God.

(GLORIA as above)

waiting for the right moment,
preparing the right way,
intending the right woman . . .
God.

(GLORIA as above)

We believe in one God,
ALL: MAKER AND MOVER OF HEAVEN AND EARTH.

Waiting
Advent meditation 1

This meditation requires six readers, three of whom should be women. The first four Readers specifically represent one of the Magi, Anna, Simeon and Mary in the nativity stories, but also more generally represent other people who looked for Jesus then and now. The Readers may stand apart on the periphery of the worship area, or come to a central speaking position. After each speaks, a response is sung and during this the Reader may – if the sight-lines allow for easy observation – place a symbol of their life on a table around a central candle. The Reader then returns to his/her place.

Personnel: *The Readers are denoted by A, B, C, D, E and F. Their symbols may be :*
A: Wise man - gold box
B: Poor widow - purse or headsquare
C: Old man - stick
D: Mother - knitting
E: Everyman - diary or keys
F: God - nappy

Suggested sung responses are I WAITED, I WAITED ON THE LORD or ON GOD ALONE I WAIT SILENTLY.

ALL: *(Sung response)*

Reader A: I am a wise man
looking for a sign.

I believe that the world is meant to be a fairer place
and that I should help to change it.
I have access to people of power and authority
but I am not sure how to use my influence.

Pray for me and for all other influential ones
who are waiting on a sign.

*(Sung response, during which Reader A
lays down their symbol)*

Reader B: I am a poor widow
looking for a purpose.

I am tired of being talked about,
treated as a statistic,
pushed to the margins of human conversation.

I want to meet someone who will have time for me,
someone who will listen to me,
someone who will not take for granted
who I am or what I have to offer.

Pray for me and for all poor people
who are waiting to be taken seriously.

ALL: *(Sung response, during which Reader B
lays down their symbol)*

Reader C: I am an old man
waiting for my death.

I have looked at the world so long
that it wearies me.
I have prayed to God so hard
for my people to be delivered
from all that diminishes and destroys them.
And I wonder, as my life closes,
if change will ever come.

Pray for me and for all older folk
who are waiting for a saviour.

ALL: *(Sung response, during which Reader C
lays down their symbol)*

Reader D: I am a young mother
waiting for my child to be born.

I feel the new life inside me,
I sense great promise throughout me,
I know my love grows
for the one I have not seen.

Yet I fear that the world may be a hostile place
for the little one who is to come.

Pray for me and for all expectant mothers
who are waiting for their child to be born.

ALL: *(Sung response, during which Reader D
lays down their symbol)*

Reader E: I am everywoman and everyman.

In my loneliness, I am waiting to be visited;
in my uncertainty, I am waiting to be reassured;
in my happiness, I am waiting for a deeper fulfilment;
in my soul, I am waiting to be wanted.

Pray for me,
and for yourself,
for we are all waiting.

ALL: *(Sung response, during which Reader E
lays down their symbol)*

Reader F: I am the Lord your God.
I have waited on you,
and have heard your prayer.

Now is the right time,
and I am coming soon.

So, prepare a way in the desert,
a cradle in the hay,
a meeting place in the market place,
a table in an upstairs room,
a cross on a hill,
a grave in a garden,
a throne in your heart as in heaven.

For now again,
I will bend down and remember you.

I will answer your prayer,
and your waiting will end in joy.

△ In the beginning of creation

Advent responses 2

Leader: In the beginning of creation,
when God made heaven and earth,
the earth was without form and void.
Darkness was over the face of the deep,
and a mighty wind swept over the waters.
God said, 'Let there be light',
and there was light.

ALL: GOD SAW THAT THE LIGHT WAS GOOD,
AND GOD SEPARATED THE LIGHT FROM DARKNESS.

Leader: When all things began, the Word already was.
The Word dwelt with God,
and what God was, the Word was.
Through him all things came to be;
no single thing was created without him.
All that came to be was alive with his life,
and that life was the light of the world.

ALL: THE LIGHT SHINES IN THE DARKNESS,
AND THE DARKNESS HAS NEVER PUT IT OUT.

(from Genesis 1 : 1-4 and John 1 : 1-5)

The people who walked
Advent meditation 2

In this prophecy (Isaiah 9: 2-7), Isaiah offers hope to his nation that God will raise up a deliverer from among them. This is no soft option, for God's deliverance is born out of love and anger, as the second section of the reading shows.

For this reading, there needs to be a confident Leader who takes the major role, and who may change position for the two monologues. If the reader can memorize the text, so much the better. Then they will be able to express with movement or gesticulation the importance of the words.

There should also be three choruses of voices who stand at different places around the circumference of the worship area. If these people can also sing the simple chord sequence under the second monologue, good and well. If they cannot, a fourth group should be identified for the sole purpose of providing the unaccompanied backing vocals.

This reading requires meticulous preparation, especially to ensure that the staggered entries such as at 'Wonderful Counsellor' synchronize well. Many sections should be spoken rhythmically, in a steady, almost rapping style. In these cases, the syllables to be stressed are shown with an acute (⋅) above them.

Personnel: **Leader**
Group A *(a chorus)*
Group B *(a chorus)*
Group C *(a chorus)*
Group D *(optional, to provide backing vocals)*

Leader: Shshshshsh . . .

Groups ALL: SHSHSHSHSH . . .

Leader: Shshshshsh . . .

Groups ALL: SHSHSHSHSH . . .

Leader:	*(Very quietly)* The people
Group A:	The people
Group B:	The people
Group C:	The people
Leader:	The péople who wálked
Group A:	The péople who wálked
Group B:	The péople who wálked
Group C:	The péople who wálked
Leader:	*(Loudly)* The péople who wálked in dárkness
Group A:	*(Less loud)* Dárkness
Group B:	*(Less loud)* Dárkness
Group C:	*(Less loud)* Dárkness
ALL:	*(Whispering repeatedly)* Dárkness, Dárkness, Dárkness *(And so on, over leader)*
Leader:	The péople who wálked in dárkness . . . have séen . . . a gréat . . . líght
ALL:	*(Changing from a whisper and gradually getting louder)* Light, Light, Light, Light. *(And so on, until leader speaks again)*
Leader:	*(Confidently)* Líght hás dáwned on thém, dwéllers in a lánd as dárk as déath. *(Gradually quickening in pace)* Yóu have increásed their jóy.

Group A:	*(Gently, but assuredly)* Wow! *(spoken as woe)*
Leader:	Yóu have gíven them gládness
Group B:	Wow!
Leader:	They rejóice as íf it were hárvest.
Group C:	Wow!
Leader:	They célebrate, júst like a párty.
ALL:	*(Loudly)* WOW!
Leader:	For you have sháttered the yóke that búrdened them.
ALL:	YES!
Leader:	You lífted the wéight from their shóulders.
ALL:	YES!
Leader:	You've remóved the táskmaster's stíck.
ALL:	YES!
Leader:	And áll the bóots of trámpling sóldiers and áll the gárments fóuled with blóod . . . thése will becóme a búrning máss; thése will becóme fuél for the fíre.
	(Pause)
Leader:	For a bóy has been bórn for us,
ALL:	BÓY BÓRN FOR US.
Leader:	A són has been gíven to us,
ALL:	SÓN GÍVEN TO US
Leader:	*(Slower)* And hé shall béar the śymbol of authórity on his shóulder; and hé shall be cálled . . .

Group A:	And hé shall be cálled . . .
Leader:	Wónderful Cóunsellor
Group B:	Wónderful Cóunsellor
Group C:	Wónderful Cóunsellor
Leader:	Míghty Gód
Group B:	Míghty Gód
Group C:	Míghty Gód
Leader:	Etérnal Fáther
Group B:	Etérnal Fáther
Group C:	Etérnal Fáther
	(Silence)
Leader:	*(Slowly)* The Prince of Peace.
	(Leader now moves position quietly)
	(Silence)
Group A:	Shshshshsh . . .
Group B:	Shshshshsh . . .
Group C:	Shshshshsh . . .
Group A:	*(Whispering)* The péople
Group B:	The péople
Group C:	The péople
Group A:	who wálked
Group B:	who wálked
Group C:	who wálked

Group A:	in dárkness
Group B:	. . . dárkness
Group C:	. . . . . . dárkness
ALL:	HAVE SEEN A GREAT LIGHT!

Leader:
(In a different mode and place)
Sháme on yóu who make únjust láws!
Sháme on yóu who oppréss my péople!
Sháme on yóu who prévent the póor
from cláiming their ríghts,
from recéiving jústice!

Sháme on yóu who thiéve from wídows!
Sháme on yóu who stéal from órphans!
Sháme on yóu who táke
from the penniless áll they háve!

Whát will you dó when you're called to accóunt?
Whére will you híde when disáster méets you?
Whó will táke you ín?
Whó will híde your weálth?

Whát will you sáy when your Gód appeárs?

Hów can an áxe claim to máster its user?
Hów can a sáw take contról of the cárpenter?
Hów can a stíck beat the pérson who hólds it?
Hów can óne with féet of cláy
defy Gód who ís etérnal?

(Leader now moves to another position)

Group A:	Shshshshsh . . .
Group B:	Shshshshsh . . .
Group C:	Shshshshsh . . .
Group A:	*(Whispering)* The people
Group B:	The people
Group C:	The people

28

Group A: who walked

Group B: who walked

Group C: who walked

Group A: in darkness

Group B: . . . darkness

Group C: . . . . . . darkness

ALL: HAVE SEEN A GREAT LIGHT!

Leader: *(Gently and intimately, natural speech rhythm, no rap)* A new branch will spring from a stump, a new king from the family of David.

ALL: *(Sing continuously and quietly)*

Leader: *(voice over)* The spirit of the Lord shall rest on him, a spirit of wisdom and understanding, a spirit of counsel and power, a spirit of knowledge and of the fear of the Lord.

He shall not judge by what he sees;
he shall not decide by what he hears;
he shall judge the poor with justice,
and defend the humble with fairness;
his mouth shall be a rod
to strike down the hard hearted
and with a word he shall silence the wicked.

Round his waist he shall wear the belt of justice;
integrity will be the cloth
wrapped round his body.

Then the wolf will lie down with the sheep,
the leopard shall lie down beside the young goat,
the calf and the lion shall grow up together . . .

(Singing stops)

and a líttle chíld . . .

Group A:	. . . and a líttle chíld
Group B:	. . . and a líttle chíld
Group C:	. . . and a líttle chíld
Leader:	And a little child shall lead them.
Group A:	Shshshshsh . . .
Group B:	Shshshshsh . . .
Group C:	Shshshshsh . . .
Group A:	*(Whispering)* The péople
Group B:	The péople
Group C:	The péople
Group A:	who wálked
Group B:	who wálked
Group C:	who wálked
Group A:	in darkness
Group B:	. . . darkness
Group C:	. . . . . . darkness
ALL:	HAVE SEEN A GREAT LIGHT

 # Among the poor
Advent litany

A:	Among the poor,
B:	among the proud,
A:	among the persecuted,
B:	among the privileged,
A:	Christ is coming,
ALL:	HE IS COMING TO MAKE ALL THINGS NEW.

A:	In the private house,
B:	in the market place,
A:	in the wedding feast,
B:	in the judgement hall,
A:	Christ is coming,
ALL:	HE IS COMING TO MAKE ALL THINGS NEW.

A:	With a gentle touch,
B:	with an angry word,
A:	with a clear conscience,
B:	with burning love,
A:	Christ is coming,
ALL:	HE IS COMING TO MAKE ALL THINGS NEW.

A:	That the kingdom might come,
B:	that the world might believe,
A:	that the powerful might stumble,
B:	that the humble might be raised,
A:	Christ is coming,
ALL:	HE IS COMING TO MAKE ALL THINGS NEW.

A:	Within us,
B:	without us,
A:	among us,
B:	before us,
A:	in this place,
B:	in every place,
A:	for this time,
B:	for all time,
A:	Christ is coming,
ALL:	HE IS COMING TO MAKE ALL THINGS NEW.

A story of light and darkness
Advent meditation 3

This meditation outlines the history of God's involvement with the ancient Jews in creation, in delivery from Egypt, and in speaking through the prophets. But rather than narrate the historical events, it identifies common elements in the experience of people today with the ancient Jews.

For the meditation, the worship space should be in comparative or complete darkness. Five Readers, with hidden torches, read their parts from the periphery of the area. A sixth person at the centre lights or extinguishes large candles which everyone should be able to see.

People should be rehearsed in the sung response they will sing, should know the spoken response, and, if need be, have words for a final song to be sung at the conclusion. Suggested sung responses are a GLORIA or BLESS THE LORD, MY SOUL from Taizé.

The reading should not be hurried, but allow space for reflection.

Personnel: **Reader A**
                Reader B
                Reader C
                Reader D
                Leader
                Candle-lighter/extinguisher

(The room is darkened)

Reader A: In the beginning,
                God allowed for chaos,
                for troubled dreams,
                and uncertain sounds,
                and fear in the darkness.

                Then, when the chaos was most threatening
                and hope was bleakest,
                God said, 'Let there be light'

ALL: AND THERE WAS LIGHT.

(A first candle is lit)

Leader: So, remember the chaos,
the uncertainty,
the confusion in which you once floundered,
and give thanks for the light.

(Silence, then a sung response)

Reader B: In the course of time,
God allowed for a journey
from ourselves to other people,
from restriction to freedom,
from a forgotten place to a promised land.

And when the journey was hardest,
and the way ahead unclear,
and the temptation to turn back most alluring,
God said, 'Let there be light'

ALL: AND THERE WAS LIGHT.

(A second candle is lit)

Leader: So, remember your journey
and how far you have travelled,
and give thanks for the light.

(Silence, then a sung response)

Reader C: Later yet,
God allowed for the special:
for friendship to grow,
for truth to be discovered,
for faith to become real.

On the mountain top
and in quiet places,
God blessed us, saying, 'Let there be light'

ALL: AND THERE WAS LIGHT.

(A third candle is lit)

Leader: So, remember not why,
but how and when and where you've been blessed,
and give thanks for the light.

(Silence, then a sung response)

Reader D: And then,
when the light was brightest,
and life was good,
despite our better judgement,
but in solidarity with all humankind,
we chased shadows,
and chose darkness.

(Candles extinguished)

Leader: So, remember how and when and where
and perhaps why you have wandered
from the light.

(Silence)

Reader A: Because God loves us,
there will be light again.

Not first in chaos,
not first on the journey,
not first for the special place,
but on the ground
and in a hidden place,
God will come,
offering a baby's hand,
to greet us.

(Sung response as candles are re-lit)

Leader: Lord Jesus Christ,
who chose, at Bethlehem, to meet us,
make us ready to lose and leave
all that makes us proud and sufficient.

Let our knees bend to you,
our hearts cradle you,
our lips sing you songs of love.

(Lights gradually come up and a carol or hymn is sung)

◯ Open our eyes
An Advent prayer 1

Open our eyes, Lord,
especially if they are half-shut
    because we are tired of looking,
or half open
    because we fear to see too much,
or bleared with tears
    because yesterday and today and tomorrow
    are filled with the same pain,
or contracted,
    because we only look at what we want to see.

Open our eyes , Lord
to gently scan the life we lead,
        the home we have,
        the world we inhabit,
and so to find,
among the gremlins and the greyness,
signs of hope we can fasten on and encourage.

Give us, whose eyes are dimmed by familiarity,
a bigger vision of what you can do
even with hopeless cases and lost causes
and people of limited ability. *(Pause)*

Show us the world as in your sight,
riddled by debt, deceit and disbelief,
yet also
shot through with possibility
for recovery, renewal, redemption. *(Pause)*

And lest we fail to distinguish vision from fantasy,
today, tomorrow, this week,
       open our eyes to one person
       or one place,
where we – being even for a moment prophetic –
might identify and wean a potential in the waiting. *(Pause)*

And with all this,
open our eyes, in yearning, for Jesus. *(Pause)*

On the mountains,
in the cities,
through the corridors of power
and streets of despair,
to help, to heal,
to confront, to convert,
O come, O come, Immanuel.

△ The desert will sing and rejoice

Advent responses 3

Leader: The desert will sing and rejoice
ALL: AND THE WILDERNESS BLOSSOM WITH FLOWERS.
Leader: All will see the Lord's splendour,
ALL: SEE THE LORD'S GREATNESS AND POWER.

Leader: Tell everyone who is anxious:
ALL: 'BE STRONG AND DON'T BE AFRAID.'
Leader: The blind will be able to see;
ALL: THE DEAF WILL BE ABLE TO HEAR;
Leader: the lame will leap and dance,
ALL: THOSE WHO CAN'T SPEAK WILL SHOUT.
Leader: They will hammer their swords into ploughs;
ALL: THEY WILL TURN SPEARS INTO PRUNING-KNIVES.
Leader: The nations will live in peace;
ALL: NO MORE WILL THEY TRAIN FOR WAR.

Leader: This is the promise of God.
ALL: GOD'S PROMISE WILL BE FULFILLED.

(from Isaiah 2:4 and 35: 1,2,5,6)

Lucky Day
Advent script 1

This is the enactment of the encounter between Zechariah and an angel.

For this script, there should be some semblance of an incense altar which can be simply represented by having a table with small holders on it into which incense sticks can be placed. This is much more advisable than running the risk of ecclesiastical offence by borrowing a regular censor.

Zechariah is totally engrossed in the activity and unaware of the approach of the angel, who may be female.

Vernacular expressions may be substituted freely.

Personnel: **Zechariah**
               Angel

Zechariah: *(Lighting incense sticks as he sings)*
                 Here we go,
                 here we go,
                 here we go,
                 here we go,
                 here we go,
                 here we go. . . oh.

                 (Stops singing and speaks to himself)

                 Oh who's the wee boy with the lucky day?

                 My first time on the incense in fifty-three years.
                 I nearly thought I was a Protestant.

                 (Lights more incense, continuing to sing)
                 Praise the Lord,
                 praise the Lord,
                 praise the Lord,

praise the Lord,
praise the Lord,
praise the Lo-ord.

(Wafting incense about)
There you go, you beauty!

Angel: *(Clears throat)*

Zechariah: *(Not looking)*
There you go . . . *(Sees angel)*
Don't tell me. It's a fairy!

Angel: I've come in answer to your prayers.

Zechariah: It's not a fairy, it's a woman!

Angel: Your prayers, not your fantasies!

Zechariah: Mercy . . . it's an angel.
Either that or it's the incense!

Here, what are you doing here anyway?
This is the holy of holies.
This is just for the high priest and honoured guests.
You should be on the other side,
watching the smoke rising.

Angel: Most of the time I am on the 'other side',
watching the smoke rising,
welcoming souls into heaven,
listening to prayers.

Zechariah: Oh . . . oh . . . , spook . . . ee . . .

Angel: Nothing spooky about it.
I'm an angel
and I've been sent by God
to you,
to tell you that your prayers have been answered.

Zechariah: Which prayers?

Angel: For a child.

Zechariah:	Oh come off it! That was years ago! Have you any idea what age Lizzie and I are? We're getting measured for our shrouds, not a christening shawl!
Angel:	God has chosen you and Elizabeth to be parents of a boy who will make you glad as well as thousands of other people.
Zechariah:	Aye, sure. My wife's an old hen, not a spring chicken. It's impossible.
Angel:	That's what you said last week about your chances of attending the incense altar . . . didn't you?
Zechariah:	How did you know?
Angel:	Listen, I was sent to bring you good news and all you've done is disbelieve me. Elizabeth is going to become pregnant. The baby is to be called John and until the child is born, you are going to be speechless.
Zechariah:	That'll be . . . *(Speechless)*
Angel:	Oh, by the way, if anyone asks you, the name's Gabriel.
Zechariah:	*(Speechless)*

△ Prepare the way of the Lord
Advent responses 4

Leader: Prepare the way of the Lord;
ALL: MAKE A PATH FOR OUR GOD IN THE DESERT.

Leader: Each valley shall be exalted;
ALL: EVERY MOUNTAIN AND HILL BE LAID LOW.

Leader: The crooked shall become straight;
ALL: ROUGH PLACES SHALL BECOME PLAIN.

Leader: The glory of the Lord shall be revealed;
ALL: ALL PEOPLE SHALL SEE IT TOGETHER.

Leader: This is the promise of the Lord;
ALL: GOD'S PROMISE SHALL BE FULFILLED.

(from Isaiah 40: 3-5)

Mary and the angel
Advent script 2

Mary should be either standing or sitting and speak directly to the audience. When Gabriel begins to speak she may interact with him or they can both simply speak to the front. The Narrator's introduction is optional.

Personnel: **Narrator** (optional)
              Mary
              Gabriel

Narrator: This is the story of what happened in the days before Jesus was born.

                In the town of Nazareth, there was a young woman whose name was Mary.

Mary: I was washing the dishes at the time.
                I was bending over the sink,
                with my back turned away from the kitchen door –
                not that he necessarily opened it.
                I just remember hearing my name being called.

Gabriel: Mary.

Mary: That's me . . .
                but who are you?
                And what are you doing here in my kitchen?

Gabriel: It's all right.
                I'm called Gabriel.

Mary: But I don't know any men called Gabriel.

Gabriel: I'm not a man.
                I'm an angel.

Mary: You don't look much like an angel to me.

Gabriel:	Have you seen an angel before?
Mary:	No. But they always have wings. Where are your wings?
Gabriel:	I don't need them when I'm not flying.
Mary:	So, what are you doing in my kitchen?
Gabriel:	I've come to bring you a message.
Mary:	You're having me on!
Gabriel:	No. I'm not. I've come to tell you that God has chosen you to enable the Incarnation to take place.
Mary:	To enable the what?
Gabriel:	The Incarnation . . . the word becoming flesh.
Mary:	Gabriel, what are you on about?
Gabriel:	You're going to become pregnant.
Mary:	Not with you, I'm not. And not in here. What do you think I am?
Gabriel:	Mary . . . it's all right. God has chosen you to become the mother of his son.
Mary:	Me? . . . I'm not even married.
Gabriel:	*(Speaking calmly)* The Holy Spirit will descend on you, and you will conceive a child, and you will call him Jesus. That means 'saviour.' Out of all the women in history, God has chosen you.

Out of all the minutes in history,
this is the one in which God needs a woman
not to give him her body,
but to give him her Yes.

Mary: *(Almost speechless)*
. . . but what will my parents say?

Gabriel: They'll be all right.

Mary: What will Joseph say?

Gabriel: Don't worry.
I'll have a word with him.

The Magnificat
Advent meditation 4

The MAGNIFICAT (Luke 1:46-55) must be one of the most frequently repeated pieces of poetry in the world. That means we run the risk of allowing it to become too familiar. The following reading, which was devised with the help of women in Milton Keynes, simply allows the promises of God contained in the text to be pondered over.

Three women are required. One is the reader who should feel confident about slowly enunciating the text in her own voice and accent. The second woman extinguishes three candles and the third places three lit candles.

Those candles to be extinguished (1A, 1B and 1C) should be large and located in prominent parts of the worship area, some distance apart from each other. The pulpit, a high ledge or ornate candle-stand are appropriate situations. When the candles are extinguished, it has to be done deliberately and, if possible, the extinguished candle should be placed on the ground. Another three candles (2A, 2B and 2C), to be placed centrally, should be small two-hour lights, and should be hidden in corners of the building where they, initially, cannot be seen. The woman who brings them forward, preferably to sit together on the altar/communion table or some other central focal point, should feel comfortable at having to walk a distance – say from the back of the church – at a slow pace, cradling the delicate flame. Because it takes a while for the humble to be lifted high, she need not hurry her movement.

The congregation, aided by a rehearsed singing group should have been introduced to two songs prior to the beginning of the service. The one (the KYRIE) is sung while the large candles are being extinguished. The other (ON GOD ALONE or MAGNIFICAT) is sung while the small candles are being brought forward.

The worst thing to do with this reading is to hurry it. If the words and action are clear and intentional, people may recognize their own history or vocation in the familiar text of the MAGNIFICAT.

Personnel: **Reader**
               Candle lighter/placer
               Candle extinguisher

My heart praises the Lord;
my soul is glad because of God my saviour,
for he has remembered me, his lowly servant!

From now on all people will call me happy
because of the great things the mighty God has done for me.

His name is holy;
from one generation to another
he shows mercy to those who honour him.

He has stretched out his mighty arm
and scattered the proud with all their plans.

(Large candle 1A doused and set aside, as KYRIE is sung)

He has brought down mighty kings
from their thrones.

(Large candle 1B doused and set aside, as KYRIE is sung)

He has lifted up the lowly.

(Small candle 2A placed, as MAGNIFICAT is sung)

He has filled the hungry with good things.

(Small candle 2B placed, as MAGNIFICAT is sung)

He has sent the rich away with empty hands.

(Large candle 1C doused and set aside, as KYRIE is sung)

He has kept the promise he made to our ancestors
and has come to the help of his servant Israel.

(Small candle 2C placed, as MAGNIFICAT is sung)

He has remembered to show mercy to Abraham
and to all his descendants forever.

| Mary, pondering
Advent reading 1

This poem may be used in Advent in relation to the experience of Mary and other women mothering their first child. It should be read by a woman who is familiar with the text. There may be some gentle chordal guitar or piano background music, and it may lead into silence and then into a prayer for all who are expecting a baby.

What is this seed which God has planted,
unasked, uncompromised, unseen?
Unknown to everyone but angels
this gift has been.

And who am I to be the mother,
to give my womb at heaven's behest,
to let my body be the hospice
and God the guest?

Oh, what a risk in such a nation,
in such a place, at such a time,
to come to people in transition
and yet in prime.

What if the baby I embody
should enter life deformed or strange,
unable to be known as normal,
to thrive or change?

What if the world, for spite, ignores him,
and friends keep back and parents scorn,
and every fear of every woman
in me is born?

Still, I will want and love and hold him,
his cry attend, his smile applaud.
I'll mother him as any mortal,
and just like God.

Mary and Lizzie
Advent script 3

*As with other similar scripts, the Narrator's introduction is optional.
There should be two seats slightly apart for the two women and
Mary begins speaking while off stage*

Personnel: **Narrator** (optional)
Mary
Lizzie

Mary: Hello, Lizzie, are you there?

Narrator: Not long after Mary was told by Gabriel
that God had chosen her to mother his son,
Mary went to see her cousin, Elizabeth.

Elizabeth was an older woman,
past child-bearing age.
But she and her husband, Zechariah,
had also been favoured by God.
Their long-forgotten prayers for a child
were being answered.

They were to become the parents
of John the Baptist,
though on account of his failure
to believe that this would happen,
Elizabeth's husband had been struck dumb
until the day of the child's birth.

Lizzie: Is that you, Mary?
Come right in.
I'm desperate for a bit of company.

Mary: *(Coming in and sitting down)*
Why?
Is nobody talking to you?

Lizzie: Well, I've noticed that several of the women
who normally pass the time of day with me,
are carefully avoiding me,
on account of my 'condition'.

Mary: That's terrible.

Lizzie: Listen, Mary,
motherhood on the other side of the menopause
doesn't make for close encounters.
I'm the talk of the neighbourhood.
And all the women keep their distance
in case they catch the same infection.

Mary: That's a lot of nonsense, Lizzie.

Martha Jacobson, the midwife,
has been touching expectant mothers
for forty years,
but it never made her pregnant.

But what about your man?
Is he not speaking to you?

Lizzie: Harry?
I'd get better conversation from a tailor's dummy.
He hasn't said a word since
I told him the 'good news'.

Mary: Is that right?

Lizzie: It is . . . but wait till I tell you this.

Last night, he plonked himself down by the fireside,
took out a pencil and paper wrote:
'Don't tell a soul, Lizzie.
The baby is to be called John.'
So I says, 'That's a funny name for a girl.'

At that the eyes nearly popped out his head.

So then I says, 'But if it's a boy,
I wouldn't want him called John.

'Just because you were called Zechariah
but changed it to Harry, it doesn't mean that every

boy wants a short handle to his jug.'
'I think I'd rather have something more exotic . . .
like . . . Shadrak . . . or Mezziboseth . . .'

Mary: What did he say to that?

Lizzie: Mary . . . he can't speak . . . remember . . .
What could he say?
He just kept pointing
to what he had written and shaking.
I thought he was going to take a seizure.

Mary: Well, apart from women not talking to you
and Harry getting upset at you,
are you all right yourself?

Lizzie: Actually, I'm quite amazed how well I am Mary.
I just occasionally have these daft turns.
Last week I had a notion
every morning when I got up
that I'd like to eat pickled herrings.

Mary: Oh, you have to expect that, Lizzie.
Some women even want to chew coal.

Lizzie: You'd need some energy for that!

Mary: Energy?
Listen, Lizzie, wait till you're in your last weeks.

There's some women become as strong as an ox.
They lift the carpets, paint the kitchen.
There's no stopping you when you're pregnant.

Lizzie: Mary, how come you know so much about it?

(Silence)

Mary?

Mary: Lizzie . . . can you keep a secret?
I think we've got something in common!

50

○ We suspect angels
Advent prayer 2

Rather than reproduce this whole prayer for congregational use, simply print the recurrent lines:

Leader: *. . . we must confess,*

ALL: *WE SUSPECT ANGELS
AND DISBELIEVE GOOD NEWS.*

Leader: Eternal God,
in the long ago days
when the earth was flat,
and heaven was above the clouds,
and disease was caused by demons,
your son was born
to lighten all our darknesses.

We now, after the enlightenment,
are in bondage to different limitations.

We doubt what we cannot prove;
we ignore what we cannot see,
and finding little room for faith,
we must confess,

ALL: WE SUSPECT ANGELS
AND DISBELIEVE GOOD NEWS.

Leader: We admit ourselves
to be both infected and affected
by the spirit of our times.

Behind talk of world peace,
we hear the machinery of war;
beneath talk of global equality
we detect the posturing of the powerful;

beside talk of your church being renewed,
we recognize the bondage to failed patterns of the
past.

Rather than embrace the light,
we become fascinated by darkness,
and must confess,

ALL: WE SUSPECT ANGELS
AND DISBELIEVE GOOD NEWS.

Leader: Ah, God,
who will save us?

Our cynicism is the fruit of our experience,
not the key to the future.
Our suspiciousness helps us to smell the rat,
never to recognize the dove.

Our perfect analysis may describe the mountain,
but is helpless to move it.

It is with little pride
we must confess,

ALL: WE SUSPECT ANGELS
AND DISBELIEVE GOOD NEWS.

Leader: As Christmas approaches,
give us a share of that divine naiveté
enjoyed by Elizabeth and Zechariah,
Mary and Joseph,
and unnamed country folk,
who encountered angels
and believed the Good News
and recognized Christ among them.

ALL: AMEN.

# △ God of the watching ones
Advent blessing

Leader: God of the watching ones,
the waiting ones,
the slow and suffering ones,
the angels in heaven,
the child in the womb,

ALL: GIVE US YOUR BENEDICTION,
YOUR GOOD WORD FOR OUR SOULS,
THAT WE MIGHT REST AND RISE
IN THE KINDNESS OF YOUR COMPANY.
AMEN.

○ Pinning our hopes on Jesus (i)
Advent intercessions

We bless you, our God,
mighty sovereign power,
gentle caring mother.
You do not forget your children.

We bless you our God,
for your great gifts to us:
creation – fragile and fascinating,
Scripture – revealing your truth.

And you bless us . . .
with your forgiving love,
with the vision of your kingdom,
shedding light in our darkness.

Bless us and disturb us God
with that vision of your kingdom,
and as we voice our hopes to you now,
                may they strengthen us,
                reassure us
                and move us . . .

We pray for those caught up in wars around the world;
soldiers, refugees and those who hold fast
to the reasons for the fighting . . .

(Silence)

We pray for homeless folk
– excluded from what the rest of us are doing,
cold, struggling to keep a hold of who they are . . .

(Silence)

We pray for folk who are ill,
coping with pain, fearing the worst,
and for those in the NHS who worry for the future . . .

(Silence)

We pray for those folk struggling in relationships,
especially at this 'family time',
when the cracks are kept just below the surface . . .

(Silence)

And for the deepest hopes of our hearts , we pray now . . .

(Silence)

Into the mess of this world a fragile child will come –
yelling in the night for his mother,
needing milk and clean linen . . .

We pin our hopes on you, little baby,
our God
– pushed out into the world,
through pain and into poverty.

Our God is with us and our hope is re-born.
AMEN.

↑ Pinning our hopes on Jesus (ii)
Advent symbolic action 1

Like CLOTH FOR THE CRADLE, page 74, this is an activity which enables people to prepare for Christmas in a symbolic way.

All that is required is four baskets to be in place throughout the worship area. Each one is lined by a nappy, folded inwards to conceal a number of nappy pins.

Before the prayer, people should be made aware of the action that follows, rather than announce the action after the prayer. They should be invited, if they wish, to move to one of the baskets as everyone sings a chant or short song (such as VENI IMMANUEL from the INNKEEPERS & LIGHT SLEEPERS collection) repeatedly. There they may take a nappy pin as a symbol of their prayers and their hope in the Christ-child.

To begin the action, the person who has led the prayer, should move as the melody of the song is played over or hummed, folding back the nappies to reveal the pins.

△ Into our world as into Mary's womb

Advent responses 5

Leader: Into our world
as into Mary's womb . . .

ALL: COME, LORD JESUS.

Leader: Into the forgotten places,
as into the stable . . .

ALL: COME, LORD JESUS.

Leader: Into the lives of the poor, bringing hope;
into the lives of the powerful, bringing caution;
into the lives of the weary, bringing rest;
into the lives of the wise, bringing restlessness;
and into our lives and longings,
whatever our estate . . .

ALL: COME, LORD JESUS.

Leader: This is the good news:
Christ is coming,
and blessed are those who wait on the Lord.

ALL: THEREFORE COME QUICKLY, LORD.
AMEN.

The village gossips
Advent script 4

The three central characters in this script must be able to interject in each other's sentences freely, as people do who are engaged in a highly participative conversation. The Narrator's lines are disposable.

Personnel: **Narrator** (optional)
Mrs Matthew
Mrs Mark
Mrs Luke

Narrator: In any small village, news travels quickly.
Therefore it is only to be expected
that the strange changes in the lives
of Mary and Elizabeth
might have been food for other
people's thought.

Mrs Matthew: Well, ladies,
you know how I'm not one for gossip,
but wait till I tell you this.

You know that old woman Elizabeth
with the man who's never spoken for nine
months.

Mrs Mark: Aye, what about her.

Mrs Matthew: They say she's had a wee boy.

Mrs Luke: At her age?
She's eighty-eight if she's a day!

Mrs Matthew: Well that's what I heard,
. . . and it was on very good authority!

Mrs Luke:	Are you sure you've got the right woman? You're not mixing her up with her cousin?
Mrs Mark:	Who? . . . Mary?
Mrs Luke:	That's her. Now, I'm not one to talk about anybody, but wait till I tell you this . . . she's pregnant.
Mrs Mark:	Never! How do you know?
Mrs Luke:	You can tell. You can just tell.
Mrs Matthew:	Oh aye, you can tell all right. I heard her in the draper's last week asking for a dress eight sizes too big for her.
Mrs Luke:	There you are . . . Draw your own conclusions. Now, I know that this will not go any further, but I hear tell that she and a certain young man are about to leave the district.
Mrs Matthew:	Who's the young man?
Mrs Luke:	The joiner's boy, . . . Joseph.
Mrs Mark:	Never!
Mrs Luke:	Well, that's what they say, and I'm not one for gossip.
Mrs Mark:	So, have you heard what they're saying about this so-called 'census'?
Mrs Matthew:	No. Tell us.
Mrs Mark:	Well, I happened to hear that the reason the Romans want our names is not to send us birthday cards.
Mrs Luke:	Well, why are they having a census?

Mrs Mark:	To register us for a Poll Tax.
Mrs Matthew:	I heard it was a 'Community Charge'.
Mrs Mark:	A rose by any other name . . .
Mrs Luke:	They wouldn't do that, would they?
Mrs Mark:	Well I'm just warning you. Mind, I'm not one for gossip.
Mrs Luke:	Nor me.
Mrs Matthew:	Nor me.

(A song should follow)

The census
Advent script 5

If this script is not introduced by the Narrator, the characters should speak from their second entry. i.e. 'So the word has come from Rome.' Note that details of a town, a neighbourhood and a bus/train route are required in the script.

The activity HOW FAR IS IT? page 64, may follow this script.

Personnel: **Narrator** *(optional)*
                Herod
                Anthony
                Brutus

Narrator: After Mary had become pregnant,
the Emperor Augustus ordered a census to be taken
throughout the Roman Empire.
All the men had to go to register
in the town where they were born.
This happened when the King in Judaea
was called Herod.

Herod: That's me.

Narrator: Herod needed to organize the census.
So he called a meeting of the generals.

**Anthony &
Brutus:** That's us.

Herod: So, the word has come from Rome
that everybody has to be registered.

Anthony: Why?

Herod: So that we can collect tax.

Brutus: What kind of tax?
Is it road tax or income tax or what?

Herod: No.
                It's what you might call a Poll Tax.

Anthony: Poll Tax? . . . that will never sell.
                Can you not get a better name?

Brutus: What about 'The Community Charge'?
                That sounds better.

Herod: All right.
                We'll call it the Community Charge.

Anthony: So do we have to go round door to door
                asking people's names?

Herod: Oh no.
                We'll not go to them.
                They'll come to us.

Brutus: What do you mean?

Herod: We'll set up a stall
                in the middle of every community
                and people will come to sign on.

Anthony: Aye, it will be the Community Charge right enough.
                The community will lynch us!

Herod: No. No.
                We'll show them who's in charge.
                We'll confuse them.

Brutus: How?

Herod: Easy . . . divide and rule.
                We'll get the head of every household
                to return to the place where he was born.

Anthony: But that means that if you were
                born in Bethlehem,
                but live in Nazareth,
                you'll have to travel seventy miles to register.

Herod: Exactly.

Brutus: And that means that if you were born in * *(insert a town at the other side of the country)* but reside in * *(insert a local neighbourhood)* you'd have to get a ** bus *(insert a bus number or details of train travel)*.

Herod: No.
Not in this census.
In this census, everybody walks to where they were born.

Anthony: And where will they live when they get there?
There's not many hotels in Bethlehem.

Brutus: There's not many hotels in ***
(insert local neighbourhood as before).

Herod: That's their problem.
Not ours.

↑ How far is it?
Advent symbolic action 2

This, and the following symbolic action, REGISTERING HOPE, page 65, can be easily used with congregations. Choose one or both.

Just to give the impression of the chaos that would be caused by a census, such as that taken before Jesus' birth, census forms, such as that illustrated below may be passed round the congregation or audience and people encouraged to tune into groups and indicate where they were born and how long it would take them to travel there on foot.

This may be concluded either by a carol or by the worship leader identifying which people live closest to their place of birth and who now lives furthest away from theirs.

CENSUS FORM

By order of his imperial majesty
CAESAR AUGUSTUS
all the world is to be taxed

Please look at the following questions and discuss your answers with your neighbours. They are intended to help you prepare for the census which will register people for taxation purposes.

You, or the head of your household, will be required to walk to the place of your birth.

a)   Where is that place?

b)   How long will it take you to travel on foot?

c)   Where can you be accommodated if the census registration involves a day or two queuing?

↑ Registering hope
Advent symbolic action 3

A further activity which may happen either after the previous symbolic activity, HOW FAR IS IT? page 64, or may be independent of it, is to have four booths set up in different parts of the worship area. These need only consist of a desk or table, above each of which should hang a sign saying NORTH, SOUTH, EAST or WEST. On the table should be a large notebook and some pens.

People are invited to consider what they deeply hope for as Christmas approaches. They are then asked – if they wish – to go to whichever booth indicates the direction of their birthplace. There, they are asked to write down what they hope for in the large notebook, either in a short sentence or as a short prayer.

After a time for reflection, they move during music or the singing of a chant or song. When everyone who wishes to has registered, four designated people should close the books and bring them to the altar or communion table, laying them open before God. The worship leader may then conclude the action with a brief prayer or collect.

Mary's journey
Advent reading 2

This monologue may be spoken by a woman after a Bible reading or before a carol which deals with the journey from Nazareth to Bethlehem.

Mary: There will be no donkey,
and especially not a 'little' donkey.

I'm eight-and-a-half months pregnant.
I couldn't swing my leg over its back.

If I sat side-saddle, I'd probably fall off
and if I stayed on, it might trigger my contractions.

Now if Joseph could afford a camel . . .
but Joseph can't afford a camel,
so I'm going to walk . . .

. . . eighty miles . . .
eighty pregnant miles
to register to pay the poll tax . . .
I don't know what it will be like
and, since Joseph left the town
when he was just a toddler,
he can't remember either.

I ask you . . .
would any of you who are women
want to walk eighty miles,
when your time has nearly come,
to give birth,
in who knows where,
to a child who is a source of consternation
to your parents before he is born
and who will be a source of controversy
to the world ever after?

When I was a girl,
I used to love playing practical jokes.
All our neighbours would roar and laugh
and say to my mother,
'Where does she get her sense of humour from?'

Sometimes when I think of the mess
that Joseph and I are in,
I smile to myself
and realize I got my sense of humour
from my maker.

The diaries of Joseph and Theodore
Advent script 6

Being an impossible reconstruction of the unkept reminiscences of the father and fiancée of a famous mother.

The two characters should be seated apart from each other. Each should have a large clipboard or notebook on which they pretend to write as they read the following lines. The characters should appear to be oblivious of each other.

Personnel: **Joseph,** *fiancé of Mary.*
Theodore, *father of Mary, husband of Anne.*

Joseph: 25th May . . . A great day.
Only one more year of my
apprenticeship to do.
Met 'M' at the dancing.
Arranged to see her next Friday.

Theodore: 25th May . . . Garden coming on.
Potatoes ready for eating.
Anne said that Mary came back all starry-eyed
about some fellow she met this evening.

Joseph: 25th June . . . I think I'm in love . . .
I think I'm in love.
I can't think of anything else.

Theodore: 25th June . . . Garden coming on,
peas ripe for picking.
Anne says Mary's very keen on this 'joiner'
she's going out with.
The lad's coming for tea next month.

Joseph: 25th July . . . Met Mary's parents.
Her mum's really nice.

Her dad's nice too,
but he can't stop talking about his garden.
He asked me if I'd build a cold frame for his lettuce.
Mary was quieter than usual
. . . maybe because we were with her parents.

Theodore: 25th July . . . Garden's doing nicely.
Beetroots need more manure.
Met Mary's boyfriend. Nice chap, a bit quiet.
Gave him a job to do
to see whether he's as good with his hands
as he's made out to be.

Joseph: 25th Aug . . . Finished building greenhouse,
garden shed and fence for Mary's dad . . .
and she said he just wanted a cold frame!
Took Mary to the seaside.
She didn't want to go into the water.
Wanted to see her in her bikini,
but she kept her jersey on all day.

Theodore: 25th Aug . . . Garden looking beautiful.
Celery the best yet.
Joseph finished the couple of jobs I gave him.
I wonder if he would do an extension
to the back lounge?
Anne asked if I saw a difference in Mary.
Reminded her
that every romance has its ups and downs . . .
reminded Anne of what it was like when we were
courting. Sometimes she wouldn't speak for weeks,
sometimes she wouldn't stop.

Joseph: 25th Sept . . . Mary's not too keen on going to
the dancing. She's stopped wearing jeans
and goes about in a dress like a bell tent.
Took her to an Indian restaurant
and she ate enough for two.

Theodore: 25th Sept . . . Garden still in good shape.
Picked a few late raspberries
for Anne to make jam.
Anne says that Mary looks overweight.
Told her it'll just be puppy fat.

Joseph: 25th Oct . . . Mary said 'Joseph would you love me

no matter what I told you?'
I said 'Yes' . . . so she told me nothing.
Her old man is dropping heavy hints
about some extension to the lounge
with a sun porch and dormer window!

Theodore: 25th Oct . . . Garden full of autumn colours.
Must pick the sprouts before the frost sets in.
Anne asked if I knew
that Mary was attending the doctor
and had I heard her knitting
in her bedroom late at night.
I told Anne that she needed to go
and see a doctor herself.
What would Mary be doing knitting
at three in the morning!

Joseph: 25th Nov . . . Mary told me she's pregnant.

Theodore: 25th Nov . . . Garden . . . oh never mind the garden!
Mary says she's in the family way.
Young folk today . . . Honestly!

Joseph: I said, 'I know it wasn't me, so who was it?'
She said it was an angel.
I said, 'Tell that to your old man!'

Theodore: I asked her if she had taken any precautions.
She said she had said her prayers.
I said that babies don't start and stop in heaven
and then she came away with this story
about an angel.
I asked her if her 'angel'
didn't happen to do a side-line
in knocking up garden sheds and greenhouses.
And she said it wasn't him. Honestly!

Joseph: What do I do?
Everybody in the village knows
and what do I say?
My boss is threatening to sack me,
my parents want to turf me out of the house
and on top of all this
I've just had a letter from the government
asking me to go back to where I was born
for something to do with a census.

Theodore: Anne, the wife, she just sits and cries all day.
Women! Honestly!

Joseph: 26th Nov . . . Went to see her parents.
He says, 'Forget about the sun lounge, son,
are you any good at knocking together a cradle?'
I said that sarcasm was the lowest form of wit
and he called me an impudent little . . .
At any rate, we've fixed a day for the wedding.
The priest says he'd do it privately.
Mary's mother says that if it's a girl,
we've to call her Senga.
Mary's father says that if it's a wee boy
we've to call it after him.
But who would want a son called Theodore?
Mary says she's got her own ideas for a name,
but it's impossible to get anything out of her.

Theodore: 26th Nov . . . Spent the day in the garden
after telling my son-in-law-to-be
what I thought of him.

Joseph: 24th Dec. . . Writing bad.
On road to my birthplace.
Mary on the donkey
saying it could be any day now.
Two miles from home.
Must stop.
Mary saying something about contractions.
What do I know about being a midwife?

The Bethel Inn
Advent script 7

This script requires five people. Deborah should speak from the back of the audience, as if she had just been talking to people at the door. It is appropriately followed by the CLOTH FOR THE CRADLE, activity, page 74.

Personnel: **Narrator**
             Innkeeper
             Miriam
             Larry
             Deborah

Narrator: Because of the census,
which required every man
to take his family to his birthplace,
Joseph took Mary to Bethlehem, a small town
which could not cope
with all its exiles now returning.

Innkeeper: This is the busiest we've ever been,
and the shortest-staffed we've ever been.

How many folk do you have cleaning the hotel, Miriam?

Miriam: Just myself.

Innkeeper: How come?
Where's Jeremiah?

Miriam: He's had to go to register at Cana.

Innkeeper: What about Martha?

Miriam: She had to go to register at Capernaum with her husband.

Innkeeper: So, are you making all the beds yourself?

Miriam: I am.
I don't want to see another pair of sheets
for as long as I live.

Innkeeper: How's the kitchen, Larry?

Larry: We're OK.
We just keep getting asked for funny food.

Innkeeper: What like?

Larry: Well, there's a couple from Syria
expect kebabs for their breakfast;
and there's an old man from the Jordan Valley
who keeps asking for locusts and wild honey.

Innkeeper: So what do you do?

Larry: I pretend I don't hear them
and give everybody a plate of porridge.

Deborah: Excuse me, are we fully booked?

Innkeeper: Absolutely, Deborah.
Standing room only!
Why do you ask?

Deborah: It's just that we've got a couple at the door,
who are desperate for somewhere to stay.
And I don't have the heart to turn them away.

Innkeeper: Well I'll tell them.

Deborah: But the woman's pregnant.
She looks as if she could have the baby any time!

Innkeeper: Deborah, we're fully booked!

Deborah: But surely there's somewhere we can put them.

Innkeeper: Where?

↑ Cloth for the cradle
Advent symbolic action 4

This is a simple liturgical activity which can happen on any of the Sundays before Christmas, allowing all who wish to make a sign of their intention to welcome Jesus.

Three orange boxes, or parts of a crib, should be in the worship space before the service begins. Over each chair or pew should be draped a strip of cloth, using as many bright colours as possible. The strips need not be more than one inch wide and fifteen inches long. Alternatively, these may be located in baskets near the centre of the worship space.

At the appropriate time, the leader uses the following or similar words, after which the musicians may play through the tune to CLOTH FOR THE CRADLE, as some children assemble the crib. When it is upright, people begin to sing and, as they wish, go out to the cradle to lay their strip of cloth over the bare wood until what looks like a patchwork quilt is made. The action and song are followed by a prayer.

Leader :   As we approach Christmas, we buy presents in preparation to give to our friends and neighbours. But how can we prepare to welcome Jesus who is at the heart of the season?

We may begin to think about that now, by joining in a very simple action.

In the centre, or, for example, at the crossing, there are pieces of wood which, if properly assembled, might make a crib or cradle.
On our chairs are strips of cloth which, if laid on top of each other, might make a patchwork quilt on which a baby could be laid.

So, let us be silent for a moment and turn our minds away from preparing for Christmas, to preparing for Jesus.

When the music plays, the crib will assembled. When we begin to sing we may, as and when we wish, come forward with our strip of cloth and lay it in the crib, symbolizing our intention to make a place and keep a welcome for Jesus.

(A short period of silence. Then music, see below, is played as the crib is assembled. Once this is done, the congregation start to sing, CLOTH FOR THE CRADLE. The song may have to be sung twice, depending on the size of the congregation, to allow people time to lay their strip of cloth on the cradle).

Chorus:
CLOTH FOR THE CRADLE, CRADLE FOR THE CHILD,
THE CHILD FOR OUR EVERY JOY AND SORROW:
FIND HIM A SHAWL THAT'S WOVEN BY US ALL
TO WELCOME THE LORD OF EACH TOMORROW.

1. Darkness and light and all that's known by sight,
   silence and echo fading,
   weave into one a welcome for the Son.
   set earth its own maker serenading.

2. Hungry and poor, the sick and the unsure,
   wealthy whose needs are stranger,
   weave into one a welcome for the Son,
   leave excess and want beneath the manger.

3. Claimant and queen, wage earners in between,
   trader and travelling preacher,
   weave into one a welcome for the Son,
   whose word brings new life to every creature.

4. Wrinkled or fair, carefree or full of care,
   searchers of all the ages,
   weave into one a welcome for the Son,
   the Saviour of shepherds and of sages.

CLOTH FOR THE CRA - DLE, CRA - DLE FOR THE CHILD, THE
FIND HIM A SHAWL THAT'S WO -VEN BY US ALL TO

dum dum etc.

CHILD FOR OUR EV - ERY JOY AND SOR - ROW.
WEL - COME THE LORD OF EACH TO - MOR - ROW. **fine**

v.1 Dark - ness and light and all that's known by sight,

ah_____

si - lence and e - cho fa - ding,

ah_____

Tune: WAE'S ME FOR PRINCE CHAIRLIE (Scots trad.)
Words and arrangement © 1987, 1997 WGRG, Iona Community, Glasgow G51 3UU, Scotland

(After all who wish to have placed their strip of cloth, the Leader may say the following prayer)

Leader: Here is a place for you, Lord Jesus.

Just as our hands have made it ready,
so make our hearts ready
to love and to welcome you.

Be born again,
not in a manger,
but in us.

Make us your Bethlehem,
where God is personal
and all things and all people
are made new.
AMEN.

△ In hope the universe waits
Advent responses 6

Leader: In hope the universe waits:
ALL: GOD'S PURPOSE SHALL BE REVEALED.

Leader: Limited by mortality,
yet destined for liberation,
in hope the universe waits:
ALL: GOD'S PURPOSE SHALL BE REVEALED.

Leader: Groaning as if in childbirth,
sampling the fruits of God's harvest,
in hope the universe waits:
ALL: GOD'S PURPOSE SHALL BE REVEALED.

Leader: Trusting in what is unseen,
believing the best is to come,
in hope the universe waits:
ALL: GOD'S PURPOSE SHALL BE REVEALED.

Leader: In the hiddenness of a byre
where the Maker of All will be born,
in hope the universe waits:
ALL: GOD'S PURPOSE SHALL BE REVEALED.

(*Adapted from Romans 8: 18-25*)

Christmas
Resources

It was to older folk that Jesus came

Christmas reading 1

This poem puts into perspective the fact that the stories of Jesus' birth deal primarily with adults. Elizabeth, Zechariah, Simeon and Anna were all evidently old. The Wise Men would not have been reputed to be wise unless they were old. And, with average male life expectancy somewhere around thirty-five years of age when Jesus was born, the Shepherds and Joseph had probably left their youth long ago.

It was to older folk that Jesus came,
that they might know their place and learn his name,
and upset notions of whom God may choose
to change the world or celebrate good news.

And this they understand who have been told
of Sarah who conceived when she was old;
and Hannah who found joy despite her tears;
and Naomi who blessed her later years.

With Zechariah, zealous for routine,
ensuring what's to come is what has been,
they may disclaim an angel's message too
declaring God intends to make things new.

Like Simeon, resigned to failing power,
old age might yet become the finest hour
for those who risk false claims that they're deranged
by saying God wants all things to be changed.

It is not in the manger Christ must stay,
forever lying helpless in the hay;
it is by older folk Jesus is blessed,
who see God's restlessness in him expressed.

△ Light looked down
Christmas responses 1

Leader: Light looked down
and saw darkness.
ALL: 'I WILL GO THERE,' SAID LIGHT.

Leader: Peace looked down
and saw war.
ALL: 'I WILL GO THERE,' SAID PEACE.

Leader: Love looked down
and saw hatred.
ALL: 'I WILL GO THERE,' SAID LOVE.

Leader: So he,
the Lord of Light,
the Prince of Peace,
the King of Love,
came down
and crept in
beside us.

1 This, tonight, is the meeting place

Christmas prologue

These words may be helpful as a prologue to a midnight mass or watchnight service, especially where those attending will not all be regular churchgoers.

This, tonight,
is the meeting place
of heaven and earth.

For this, tonight,
is the stable
in which God keeps his appointment
to meet his people.

Not many high are here,
not many holy;
not many innocent children,
not many worldly wise;
not all familiar faces,
not all frequent visitors.

But, if tonight
only strangers met,
that would be enough.

For Bethlehem was not the hub of the universe,
nor was the stable a platform for famous folk.

In an out-of-the-way place
which folk never thought to visit –
there God kept and keeps his promise;
there God sends his son.

The journey of Jesus
Christmas reading 2

These words are based on Psalm 139 and here used with reference to Christ in the womb, about to come into the world. It should be read in darkness, especially at a midnight service, with the following or a similar introduction.

Leader: As we prepare to celebrate the birth of Jesus,
let us feel for him as the unseen child in the
womb, sensing that the time for him
to leave the place of safety was near.
We do not know what his thoughts would be,
but the words of Psalm 139
might help us imagine them.

Reader: Lord, you have examined me and you know me.
You know me at rest and in action;
you understand my thoughts from far away.
You trace where I will travel and where I will rest.
You are familiar with the paths I will have to take.

You created me inside and out;
you have knitted me together in my mother's womb.
My body is no mystery to you;
you formed me in secret,
you wove me in the depths of the earth,
you have shaped me and foreseen my actions
before I come into being.

And soon I am to be born,
to leave the silence and security of the womb
for the uncertainty of the world.

Into your hands I commit my spirit,
and ask you to commend my life
into the hands of those
who will want me,

welcome me,
feed me,
clothe me,
listen to me,
sing for me.
Knowing that I might be abused,
ignored,
undernourished,
abandoned,
knowing that you will not deny me danger,
into your hands I commit my spirit,
and into the hands of strangers
I present my self.

☐ The Incarnation
Christmas script 1

This script may be used in complete absence of movement, simply by positioning the three voices in different parts of the hall or church and having the dialogue appropriately interspersed with simple lines of music. This would allow for evocative slides to be shown to accompany the words.

More commonly, the script has involved groups of people miming actions in keeping with the words of the two Narrators while the person representing God sits aloof on a ladder and eventually comes down to the world in the closing sentences.

In either case, the sketch is best followed immediately by a song, preferably beginning before the actors or readers leave the stage. BEFORE THE WORLD BEGAN from the HEAVEN SHALL NOT WAIT collection is most suitable.

Personnel: **Narrator A**
Narrator B
Narrator C
God
Prophets *(who may also mime actions as appropriate)*

Narrator A: God looked around and saw the world
which he had made a long time ago.
And what he saw upset him.

In one place
preachers were talking about peace,
priests were talking about peace,
prophets were talking about peace.
So much talking,
but there was no peace.
There was only talking to hide the noises of war.

God sighed a heavy sigh.

(God sighs)

Narrator B: In another place
people were building,
building banks and storehouses,
building monuments to their own greed,
building meat mountains and butter mountains.
So much building,
while the poor became poorer
and the scales of justice were biased to the rich.

God sighed a heavy sigh.

(God sighs)

Narrator A: In another place
people were doing their own thing,
doing their own thing about loving,
doing their own thing about trusting,
doing their own thing about healing.
So much doing their own thing,
but the truth was
that nothing was being done,
for all were divided, suspicious and lonely.

God sighed a heavy sigh.

(God sighs)

Narrator B: In another place,
people were worshipping,
worshipping what their hands had made,
worshipping what their money had bought,
worshipping what their fantasies had imagined.
So much worshipping,
but no faith and no hope and no God.

God sighed a heavy sigh.

(God sighs)

Then he stopped sighing and got angry,
and said . . .

God: I'm fed up.
There's only one answer to this mess –
I'm going to destroy the world!

Narrator A: Then God thought for a minute
and he began to cry.
And through the tears he said . . .

God: How can I kill those who were born out of my love?
I am God, not a man.
I will not destroy.
I will save the world.
I will let the world know that I love it.

Narrator A: So God got to thinking:

God: How can I tell my people that I love them?

Narrator A: God's first thought was telepathy.

God: I'll just think about it.
I'll sit down and think about it
and if they read my thoughts,
they'll know how I feel.

Narrator A: So God sat down and thought and thought,
but people had other things on their minds.

God: So much for telepathy . . .

Narrator A: said God.

Narrator B: God's second thought was sign language.

God: I'll make some signs to show that I love them,
then they'll understand
and things will turn for the better.

Narrator B: So God made some signs . . .
like . . . a rainbow.

God: *(Sings)* 'Somewhere over the rainbow . . .'

Narrator B: But nobody understood.
Then he made another sign
by opening the Red Sea
to let his people escape from slavery.

God: *(Sings)* 'If you go down to the sea today,
you're sure of a big surprise . . .'

Narrator B: And the people were impressed,
but nobody really understood.

Then he made another sign:
he gave them food in the desert.

God: *(Sings)* 'Food glorious food,
cold manna for breakfast . . .'

Narrator B: And everybody ate,
but nobody really understood.
Nobody understood any of God's signs.

God: So much for sign language . . .

Narrator B: said God.

Narrator A: God's third thought was telegrams.
For these he needed messengers
whom he called prophets.

And they each received telegrams,
some with few words, some with many words.
They were to read these to the people.

Prophets: *(Or Narrator B)*
Words, words, words, words, words.

Narrator A: But, for all the words,
nobody understood;
or, if they did,
they didn't let on.

God: So much for telegrams . . .

Narrator A: said God.

Then God thought about using the telephone,
but when he discovered the cost
of long distance calls,
he decided not to bother.

God sighed a heavy sigh.

(God sighs)

Narrator B: Then God had a brainwave.

God: I'll send . . .
I'll send . . .
I'll go there myself . . . but how?

Narrator A: God called a meeting of his three selves . . .
the Creator, the Word and the Spirit.

God: I move the Word goes,

Narrator B: said the Creator.

God: *(Using a different accent)* I second that.

Narrator B: said the Spirit.

God: *(Using a different accent)* Wait a minute !

Narrator B: said the Word.

Narrator A: But there was no minute,
for there was no time.
So the Word became flesh:
tiny and frail flesh,
nappy wet and girning flesh,
bone of our bone,
flesh of our flesh,
the son of Joseph and Mary.

Litany of the Incarnation
Christmas litany

This litany may be read after the reading of the Christmas Gospel or after the announcement of Christmas Day. In each case it should be read positively and may lead to a song celebrating the Incarnation of Jesus.

Leader: When the time was right, God sent the Son;
Women: sent him and suckled him,
Men: reared him and risked him,
Women: filled him with laughter and tears and compassion,
Men: filled him with anger and love and devotion.

Leader: Unwelcomed child, refugee and runaway,
ALL: CHRIST IS GOD'S OWN SON.

Leader: Feeder and teacher, healer and antagonist,
ALL: CHRIST IS GOD'S OWN SON.

Leader: Lover of the unlovable,
toucher of the untouchable,
forgiver of the unforgivable,
ALL: CHRIST IS GOD'S OWN SON.

Leader: Loved by women, feared by men,
befriended by the weak, despised by the strong,
deserted by his listeners, betrayed by his friends,
bone of our bone, flesh of our flesh,
writing heaven's pardon over earth's mistakes,
ALL: CHRIST IS GOD'S OWN SON.

Leader: The Word became flesh:
ALL: HE CAME AMONG US,
HE WAS ONE OF US.

◯ When the world was dark
Christmas intercessions 1

This prayer may be read as below, or may be interspersed with moments of silence or the singing of a chant such as O LORD, HEAR MY PRAYER from Taizé.

When the world was dark
and the city was quiet,
you came.

You crept in beside us.

And no-one knew.
Only the few
who dared to believe
that God might do something different.

Will you do the same this Christmas, Lord?

Will you come into the darkness of today/tonight's world;
not the friendly darkness
as when sleep rescues us from tiredness,
but the fearful darkness,
in which people have stopped believing
           that war will end
           or that food will come
           or that a government will change
           or that the Church cares?

Will you come into that darkness
and do something different
to save your people from death and despair?

Will you come into the quietness of this city/town,
not the friendly quietness
as when lovers hold hands,
but the fearful silence
           when the phone has not rung,

the letter has not come,
the friendly voice no longer speaks,
the doctor's face says it all?

Will you come into that darkness,
and do something different,
not to distract, but to embrace your people?

And will you come into the dark corners
and the quiet places of our lives?

We ask this not because we are guilt-ridden
or want to be,
but because the fullness our lives long for
depends on us being as open and vulnerable to you
as you were to us,
when you came,
wearing no more than nappies,
and trusting human hands
to hold their maker.

Will you come into our lives,
if we open them to you
and do something different?

When the world was dark
and the city was quiet
you came.

You crept in beside us.

Do the same this Christmas, Lord.
Do the same this Christmas.
AMEN.

The shepherd
Christmas script 2

This short monologue should be read by a young person of twelve years old or over, who could be the kind of apprentice alluded to in the words. The Narrator's part may be omitted if required.

Personnel: **Narrator** *(optional)*
                Shepherd

Narrator: At the time of Jesus' birth,
shepherding was not the romantic profession
it is often presumed to be.
It meant staying awake at night
to ward off wolves or thieves.
It also meant being unable
to attend every religious service,
if a deputy could not be found.

It is therefore interesting
that the first people to hear of God's great gift
were those who would not always be in church.

Shepherd: It's kind of difficult to explain, Mr Cohen . . .
and I can well understand why you're angry . . .
I mean to say . . .
I would be angry too if I were in your position.

I know I've only been working with you for a week.
But I can assure you
it's not the kind of thing I do often.
I always stay on the job.

But what I said is perfectly true . . .
you can ask Larry or Samuel . . .
admittedly, it does seem a bit incredible . . .

I mean there were noises in the sky . . .
musical noises, and we did go to the village . . .

just the three of us, and . . .
and there was a baby . . .
a boy . . .
and we weren't drunk . . .
just a bit emotional.

OK . . . that doesn't explain where the sheep got to.
And I know it's highly unusual
for Goldberg the butcher to be selling lamb
at bargain prices.

But, Mr Cohen there are some things in life
more important than sheep . . .

No, I don't want to go into the priesthood,
I want to be a shepherd.
But shepherds can believe in God too, can't they?

And did it happen?
Christmas reading 3

This is the text for a song of the same name which can be adequately read as a poem celebrating the Nativity. The music can be found in the INNKEEPERS AND LIGHT SLEEPERS collection.

And did it happen
that in a stable long ago,
a weary couple,
who no-one wanted to know,
should choose a manger,
in spite of the danger,
to hold and hallow the Lord below?

And did it happen
that in the stillness of the night,
the woman laboured
to let God see the light,
and bathed and dressed him,
breastfed and blessed him,
the Word incarnate whose time was right?

And did it happen
that news of this first reached the poor,
compelled by angels
to tiptoe to the door
and see no trappings,
just linen wrappings,
a baby for certain and God for sure?

And did it happen
that all of this was meant to be,
that God from distance
should choose to be set free
and show uniqueness
transformed in weakness,
that I might touch him and he touch me?

△ They have heard it on the hills

Christmas proclamation

To be read by two voices, with the possibility of the congregation singing a GLORIA between and following the reading with a carol or hymn.

Leader 1:   They have heard it on the hills,
they have heard it in the streets;
the rumour prevails,
and none can contradict it.

Leader 2:   Some are looking up the prophets,
some are studying the skies,
others speculate or calculate,
but none deny the facts.

Leader 1:   Some are dancing back to sheepfolds,
some are travelling foreign roads,
some await more information,
others celebrate the news.

Leader 2:   In a foreign place,
a ruler has imposed a new tax,
in a hilly place,
an old woman suckles her new son,
in a royal place,
an old ruler senses a new threat,
in a busy place,
a young couple cope with their new child,

Leader 1:   At what seems the wrong time,
in what seems the wrong place,
among those who seem the wrong people,
God has decided to bless,
          disturb
          and visit us.

The Word
Christmas meditation 1

This is a straightforward reading of part of the prologue to John's Gospel (John 1: 1-5 and 1: 10-14), with a sung response interspersed. The sung response, BE STILL AND KNOW, requires a singing Group to hold a straightforward chord progression over which the congregation ultimately sings a melody in canon. The congregation should rehearse before the service and a cantor should bring them in, at the last singing. The first four times the sung response occurs involves the Group singing their part through twice.

The drama may be heightened by having someone place an open Bible, a candle and a cross on a central location at the appropriate times.

Personnel: **Reader**
                   Group *(to sing chord progression)*
                   Bible/Candle/Cross-placers *(optional)*

Group: *(Sung response – BE STILL AND KNOW)*

Reader: In the beginning was the Word
                  and the Word was with God
                  and the Word was God.

                  The Word was with God at the beginning
                  and through him all things were created.
                  No created thing came into being without him.

Group: *(Sung response – an open Bible may be placed)*

Reader: In the Word was life,
                  and that life was the light of humankind.
                  The light shines in the darkness,
                  and the darkness has never put it out.

Group: *(Sung response – a lit candle may be placed)*

Reader: He was in the world;
but the world – though it owed its being to him –
did not recognize him.
He came to his own,
and his own people would not receive him.
But to those who did receive him,
he gave the right to become children of God,
not through human desire, but through God alone.

Group: *(Sung response – a cross may be placed or a
symbol of a baby such as a nappy or bottles)*

Reader: So, the Word became flesh;
he came among us and was one of us.
And we saw his glory,
the glory which befits God's only son,
full of grace and truth.

**Group
(then ALL):**   *(Sung response – after the Group has sung
their part twice, the cantor should bring in the
congregation to sing the melody in harmony
continuously).*

☐ A perfect disgrace
Christmas script 3

Like THE VILLAGE GOSSIPS, page 58, this script deals with the kind of street corner conversation or tabloid press reporting in which scandal is all important. It may be preceded by the words from St John's Gospel, given to the Narrator.

Personnel: **Narrator**
A
B
C

Narrator: The Word was in the world,
but the world, though it owed its being to him,
did not recognize it.
He came to his own,
but his own would not receive him.

A: It's a perfect disgrace!

B: It's a pure liberty!

C: It's a scandal!

A: She was pregnant before they got married.

B: She was not!

C: She was!

A: It's a perfect disgrace!

B: It's a pure liberty!

C: It's a scandal!

A: Of course, you know the only reason why they got married?

B: No, what was it?

A: To prevent folk from talking.

C: As if folk can't put two and two together.

A: It's a perfect disgrace!

B: It's a pure liberty!

C: It's a scandal!

A: Did you hear that he'd given up his job?

B: No!

A: Yes, he did . . . and they've moved away.

C: With her in that condition?

A: Exactly!

A: It's a perfect disgrace!

B: It's a pure liberty!

C: It's a scandal!

A: Do you know what I've just heard?

B: Tell me.

A: They're saying that the Word became flesh.

C: Get away!

A: That's what they're saying.

A: It's a perfect disgrace!

B: It's a pure liberty!

C: It's a scandal!

Michael Mouse
Christmas script 4

MICHAEL MOUSE moved from being a children's story to a radio play to a script for voices and optional action. Sometimes it has been presented with children playing in full costume, sometimes in darkness with the characters wearing masks appropriate to the animals they represent and the nativity scene momentarily lit from behind a screen, so that shadows of Mary and Joseph are seen by the audience. Users of this script should feel free to be flexible. Hence there are no indications of movement.

Some of the Narrator's lines appear in brackets. This indicates that, in the case of the play being enacted, these lines might better be omitted.

Personnel: **Narrator**, *preferably seated with a story book in an easy chair.*
Michael Mouse
Owl
Sheep
Cow
Hen
Cat
Joseph, *off-stage.*
Chorus *of the above characters or other voices to hum carols.*

Narrator: A long, long time ago,
on the night when Jesus was born,
there was a wee mouse called Michael.

Now I hope you're not afraid of wee mice,
because this was a very friendly one.

He had big ears and a long tail, tiny wee eyes
and a red boiler suit (*or* red woolly jacket)
to keep out the cold.

He was sleeping in a wee hole
just above a burn (*or* stream)
thinking nice thoughts and making nice noises.

Michael: *(Snores)*

Narrator: Suddenly he was wakened by a strange noise.
He looked up into the sky
and saw that it was bright, bright as day
though it was the middle of the night.
And then he heard . . .

Others: *(Sing or hum HARK THE HERALD ANGELS)*

Narrator: Michael thought he would like to find out
what the singing was all about,
so he scampered along to see a good friend of his,
an owl, who lived up a tree
and had a good view of everything that went on.

Owl: Tu-wit-tu-woo, tu-wit-tu-woo.

Michael: What's all the noise about?

(Narrator: asked Michael, and the owl replied:)

Owl: There's a great commotion,
all because a little baby has been born
in the village of Bethlehem.
Everybody's going to see him, so it seems.

Michael: Bethlehem! That's miles away.
Do you think it's worth me going too?

Owl: Oh, I'm sure you would find it
a memorable experience.
Tu-wit-tu-woo, tu-wit-tu-woo.

Narrator: So, off went Michael.
There weren't any buses or trains in these days,
so he had to swim across two rivers
and climb hills all on his own.
There was a long way to go.

Michael: *(Panting noises – especially if Michael has been
running around)*

Narrator: At last he arrived and he stood in the yard

just next to the stable where Jesus was born.
He was quite exhausted and his wee red boiler suit
(*or* red jacket) was all dirty.
So he gave himself a lick
to clean himself up as best he could.

Michael: *(Slurping noises)*

Narrator: After all,
he wanted the wee baby to see him at his best.
While he was sorting himself along came . . .

Sheep: Baaa . . . baaa . . . baaa . . .

Narrator: Along came some sheep.

Michael: Hello you . . . I mean . . . Mrs Ewe . . .

(**Narrator**: Michael said to one of the mummy sheep.)

Michael: Where are you going?

Sheep: Aaahhm goooing to seee the weee baaaby.

Michael: Can I come with you?

(**Narrator**: asked Michael thinking he'd get a good view
if he stood on the sheep's shoulders.)

Sheep: Haaave you got a preeeseeent?

Michael: No.

(**Narrator**: answered Michael,
for he didn't think of bringing a present.)

Sheep: Then you caaan't cooome with meee.

Michael: What kind of present have you got, Mrs Ewe?

Sheep: I've got some woool
to keeep the weee baaaby waaarm . . .
Baaa . . . baaa . . . baaa . . .

Narrator: . . . and into the stable walked Mrs Ewe and her friends.
As they left, Michael heard another sound.

Cow:	Mooo . . . mooo . . . mooo . . .
Michael:	Well, hello, Mrs Coo . . . sorry, Mrs Cow, how do you dow? . . . I mean do? And where are you off to?
Cow:	Moo . . . moo . . . I'm not off anywhere. I'm here to see the wee baby.
Michael:	Would you give me a wee ride on your back so that I can see him too?
Cow:	Moo . . . moo . . . do you have a present?
Michael:	No.
Cow:	Then you cannot come too.
Michael:	What kind of present have you got, Mrs Cow?
Cow:	I've got some milk in case the wee baby gets thirsty. Moo . . . moo . . .
Narrator:	So Mrs Cow moo-mooed her way into the stable. Michael was quite sad. He could not get in and he was especially sad when he heard how the people inside were enjoying themselves.
Chorus:	*(Hum GOD REST YE MERRY, GENTLEMEN)*
Michael:	*(Joins in carol to 'La')*
Narrator:	Michael was la-laaing away to himself when he heard another visitor.
Hen:	Cluck-cluck, cock-a-doodle, cluck-cluck.
Michael:	Well, hello, hen.
Hen:	Mrs Hen to you, son, if you don't mind.
Michael:	OK, OK. Don't get your feathers ruffled. I'm surprised to see you here, all the same.

Hen: Cluck-cluck.
No surprise at all.
This isn't the first maternity ward I've visited.
I like to see babies just as much as anyone else.
Cluck-cluck.

Michael: That's why I'm here,
just in case you were wondering.
What are the chances of us going in together?
You see, I don't know anybody.

Hen: Have you a present for the wee baby?

Michael: No, I don't.

Hen: Well, you can't come with me.
At least I've brought some eggs with me.
That's my gift to the child.

Michael: But I don't see any eggs.

Hen: That's because I haven't laid them yet.
Cluck-cluck.

Narrator: . . . and away she clucked into the stable.

Michael got sadder and sadder.
He was determined to get in,
but he didn't know how.
So he thought he'd walk around for a bit
and eventually he found himself
right outside the stable door.
He looked up and you'll never guess
what was staring him straight in the face . . .

Cat: Meeaouw . . . meeaouw . . .

Narrator: It was a big cat.

Cat: Meeaouw . . .

Narrator: It was a big ginger tom cat with smelly breath.
It had been eating a fish supper (*or* a tin of sardines)
and it hadn't cleaned its teeth.
It breathed right into Michael's face.

106

Cat: *(Here, as elsewhere, CAT should speak in a strong local accent. Amend to suit.)*
Jist whit are you efter?

Michael: *(Frightened)*
I'm just here to see the wee baby, honest.

Cat: Yer jist here to see the wee baby, eh?
Huv you goat a present fur the wee baby?

Michael: No, I haven't.

Cat: Well, yer no gettin' in.

Michael: But what about you?
You don't have a present for the wee baby?
What are you doing in the stable?

Cat: Ahm employed tae keep wee gomerels
(*or* hooligans) like you far, far away. Take this!

Narrator: And at that the cat went to hit Michael
with his big ginger paw.
But Michael scampered
and ran to the side of the stable
where he puffed and puffed,
breathless with fear and excitement.

While he was puffing and panting,
he saw some other visitors to the stable,
not hens or sheep or cows,
but other ones . . . you know who . . .

Chorus: *(Play, hum or sing THE FIRST NOWELL or AS WITH GLADNESS)*

Narrator: So there was Michael.
He'd run all the way,
he'd got his clothes dirty,
he'd talked to the visitors going in,
he'd heard the singing inside,
he'd been threatened by a maladjusted tom cat.
And he couldn't . . . he couldn't get in.

Michael was sad.
He was very, very sad,
and he began to cry.

Michael: *(Sobs)*

Narrator: A big tear dribbled down to the end of his wee nose
and on to his boiler suit (*or* red jacket) . . .
he was so sad.

I don't know what it was,
but something made him look up.
He looked up to the stable wall and, though it was
very dark, he saw a chink of light
about the size of a ten pence piece.
It was a wee hole.
And Michael wondered
if he could maybe climb up to it.
It was very high and as he climbed higher and higher
the wind got louder and louder.

Chorus: *(Wind noises)*

Narrator: It was blowing a gale
by the time he reached the hole.
First he squeezed his head in.

Michael: *(Squeeze noise)*

Narrator: Then he squeezed his body in.

Michael: *(Squeeze noise)*

Narrator: And then he went headfirst into the hole
and stuck his bottom in it
and let his tail dangle down outside.

It took him a wee while to get used to the light,
because it was quite bright in the stable.
But as soon as his eyes were all right,
the first thing he noticed
was that Mary, the baby's mother,
was looking over at him.
She gave him a big wink.
Then she got Joseph, the wee baby's father
to look over at Michael.
And he gave him a big wink and then said,
ever so gently,

Joseph: Thanks, wee man.

Narrator: That puzzled Michael.
Why should Joseph thank him?
And then he realized what he had done.
You see that hole in the wall
was too high for Joseph to reach up and plug it,
and he and Mary were worried
in case Jesus would feel the draught
and catch a cold.

Of course the moment Michael plonked his bottom
in the hole,
the draught stopped.
Mary didn't have to worry any longer,
so in Michael's honour she sang a wee lullaby.

Chorus: *(Hum or 'La, La' LITTLE JESUS SWEETLY SLEEP or other lullaby)*

Narrator: Oh, Michael was really chuffed (*or* thrilled).
And he felt especially pleased
now that he had a bird's-eye view
. . . though it was really a mouse-eye view.
He could see everything.

He saw the sheep giving their wool
to keep the wee baby warm.

Sheep: Baaa . . . baaa . . .

Narrator: He saw the cow giving her milk to the baby
when he was thirsty.

Cow: Moo . . . moo . . .

Narrator: Then he saw the hen laying her eggs . . .
and, since she wasn't sure whether it was right
to give eggs to such a wee baby,
she gave them to Mary instead.

Hen: Cluck-cluck.

Narrator: And he saw the shepherds and the wise men
give their presents

and everybody looked so happy,
even the big ginger tom cat with the smelly breath.

Cat: Meeaouw.

Narrator: Michael stayed in the hole in the wall
all night until the morning came.
Then, when the wind had stopped howling,
and without any fuss,
he climbed down the outside wall
and headed for home.

By the time he got back to the burn (*or* stream)
where he lived, he was very tired.

Michael: *(Yawning noise)*

Narrator: But his friend was there waiting to greet him.

Owl: Tu-wit-tu-woo . . . I've heard all about it, you know.

I've spoken to the sheep,
I've had a word with the cow,
I listened for ages to one of the hens.

They told me all about it. And they told me
how you didn't get in to see the baby
because you didn't have a present for him.

Michael: Oh yes, I did see the baby!

Chorus: But I thought you didn't have a present.
What did you give him?

Michael: I gave him me for as long as he needed me.

Narrator: Then Michael turned and disappeared
into his wee hole at the side of the burn.

And that is where the story ends,
with Michael's words . . .
'I gave him me, for as long as he needed me.'
There's no better gift to give Jesus
today or any day.

☐ A special baby
Christmas script 5

The dialogue between Mary and Joseph can be read from out of sight of the congregation or audience, as if they were eavesdropping on a conversation in the next room. The Narrator's lines may be omitted.

Personnel: **Narrator** *(optional)*
Mary
Joseph

Narrator: Both Mary and Joseph had been told by an angel
of the importance of their child.
But both were also parents for the first time
and there is no reason to believe
that parenting was second nature.

Mary: Eh . . . Joseph . . . Joseph!

Joseph: *(As if walking up)*
Uh . . . what it is, Mary?

Mary: Can you not hear anything?

Joseph: No, I was sleeping, Mary.

Mary: Well, listen.
(Pause)
Listen!

Joseph: I'm listening!

Mary: Well, can you not hear the baby crying?

Joseph: Oh, is that what it is?
Yes, I hear it loud and clear, Mary.

Mary: So?

Joseph: So?

Mary: So, what do you think that means, Joseph?

Joseph: It means he's not sleeping, Mary.

Mary: Neither am I, Joseph.
But why is he not sleeping?

Joseph: He's needing fed, maybe.

Mary: I gave him his feed half an hour ago.

Joseph: So?

Mary: So, what else could it be?

Joseph: A dirty nappy, maybe?

Mary: Ten out of ten, Joseph.
(Pause)
So?

Joseph: So . . . somebody will have to change him, Mary.

Mary: And whose turn might it be, Joseph?

Joseph: Oh, not me again, Mary.
I thought this was a special baby.
I thought the angel said it was to be God's son!

Mary: That's right, Joseph.
But even God's son needs his nappies changed.

Once in Judah's least known city

Christmas reading 4

This is a deliberate parody on a better-known carol, and should be read rather than sung. It provides a small antidote to those sentimental trappings of the season, which sometimes hide the risk and rawness of the Incarnation.

Once in Judah's least known city
stood a boarding house with back-door shed,
where an almost single-parent mother
tried to find her new-born son a bed.
Mary's mum and dad went wild
when they heard their daughter had a child.

He brought into earth a sense of heaven:
Lord of none and yet the Lord of all;
and his shelter always was unstable
for his mission was beyond recall.
With the poor, with those least holy,
Christ the King was pleased to live so lowly.

Can he be our youth and childhood's pattern
when we know not how he daily grew?
Was he always little, weak and helpless,
did he share our joys and problems too!
In our laughter, fun and daftness
does the Lord of love suspect our gladness!

Not in that uncharted stable
with the village gossips standing by
but in heaven we shall see him –
which may not be up above the sky –
if, in love for friend and stranger,
we embrace the contents of the manger.

△ A boy has been born for us
Christmas responses 2

Leader: A boy has been born for us;
ALL: A CHILD HAS BEEN GIVEN TO US.

Leader: And his name shall be called
Wonderful Counsellor, Mighty God,
Eternal Father, the Prince of Peace.
Once we were no people;
ALL: NOW WE ARE GOD'S PEOPLE.

Leader: Once we walked in darkness;
ALL: NOW WE HAVE SEEN A GREAT LIGHT.

(from Isaiah 9: 2,6 and 1 Peter 2: 10)

In the face of the Gospel
Christmas intercessions 2

A short KYRIE or other response may be sung after each petition. Or there may be a spoken response such as, 'LORD HAVE MERCY', or 'LORD, HEAR US, LORD, GRACIOUSLY HEAR US.'

In the face of the Gospel,
let us ask God for a good Christmas:

. . . that no powerful nation
     should tax the poor
     or uproot them;

. . . that no unmarried mother
     should be put away in disgrace;

. . . that no door will be shut
     on those who need to find it open;

. . . that shepherds and sheep and all of nature
     need not be afraid;

. . . that barbed wire and angry soldiers
     may not be found in Bethlehem;

. . . that wise men and wise women
     might appear in Belfast,
                    in East Timor,
                    in Lima

. . . that children may be preserved
     from those who would abuse them;

. . . that this Christmas,
     worship may become a manger
     and the church a stable,
     and the rumour become a reality
     that Christ has come among us.

And this we pray in Jesus' name.
AMEN.

☐ Anna and Simeon
Christmas script 5

Two older people should be asked to read this dialogue, which they can do, sitting side by side on a bench. The Narrator's lines may be omitted.

Personnel: **Narrator** *(optional)*
Simeon
Anna

Narrator: It was the custom of Jewish parents
to go to the Temple in Jerusalem
and there dedicate their child.
When Mary and Joseph did this,
they were greeted by two elderly people,
Simeon and Anna.
They had been waiting and praying
for God to send the Messiah,
and recognized that their prayers
had been answered.

Not for the first time,
God uses older people
to be the midwives of a new age.

Simeon: Anna . . .

Anna: Simeon?

Simeon: I thought I would wait on you.

Anna: Have you been waiting long?

Simeon: Seventy years.

Anna: So have I.
(Pause)
Are you sure?

Simeon: Are you sure?

Anna: Yes . . . I saw him.

Simeon: Anna, I held him.
I held him in the crook of my arm,
and let this wrinkled hand touch his brow
and I felt young again.
Yes . . . I'm sure.

Anna: You spoke to them?

Simeon: Yes, to her more than him.
I told her what I was told to tell her.

Anna: How did she take it?

Simeon: With tears in her eyes.
How else?
Who wants to hear about death so close to birth?
She took it like one who knew
that through her child
the best and worst will change place
all the time.

Anna: What now?

Simeon: A bottle of wine and a loaf from the baker's.

Anna: Can I join you?

Simeon: I was just going to ask you.

Women weeping
Christmas meditation 2

The commemoration of the Holy Innocents is a time when we may remember children and young people whose lives have been sacrificed in war or persecution or lost through misfortune, illness, or abuse. In such a poignant time of remembering, people may wish to make a sign of those for whom they grieve – whether that be children they have lost, or the children of other nations slaughtered in war or through persecution. To enable this to happen, some alternative symbolic action is possible. People may each bring, or be given, a flower which, at the appropriate time they lay at the foot of a cross. Or there may be one or more open books in whose pages names may be written. Or there may be an area at the foot of a cross, icon or picture where a large candle burns, from which smaller votive candles may be lit.

It is important, before worship begins, to let people know what the symbolic action is and to say that such action is completely optional. Similar words should be repeated before this meditation begins and not in the middle, after the dialogue has ended. Thus there can be an easy flow from word to action.

The sung response BE STILL AND KNOW may be appropriately sung during the symbolic action.

Personnel: **Leader**
            Voice 1
            Voice 2
            Voice 3

Leader: A voice was heard in Ramah,
            sobbing and loudly lamenting:
            it was Rachel weeping for her children,
            refusing to be comforted
            because they were no more.

Voice 1:   And many had wept before her:
            mothers of Israel,

captive in Egypt,
afraid to give birth to a boy,
lest he be slaughtered
because Pharaoh was threatened.

Voice 2:   And many wept with her,
mothers of Israel,
whose children had been exiled,
driven from their birthplace
on account of their sin
and the sin of their fathers before them.

Voice 3:   And many have cried after her,
mothers of Israel,
their homeland occupied,
afraid for the boys they had borne,
lest they be slaughtered
because Herod was threatened.

Leader: A voice was heard in Ramah,
sobbing and loudly lamenting:
it was Rachel weeping for her children,
refusing to be comforted
because they were no more.

Voice 1:   And many still cry,
the mothers of Nicaragua
and El Salvador
and Guatemala
and all who dance alone,
whose sons and husbands,
at night or dawn or in broad daylight,
were made to disappear.

Voice 2:   And others still cry,
the mothers of Israel
and Palestine
and Lebanon
and Syria
caught up in a holy war
which sacrifices their children.

Voice 3:   And others still cry,
the mothers of Angola
and Mozambique
and Vietnam,

whose children born after the battles,
are maimed by British landmines.

Voice 1: And still they cry,
for their silent sons and silenced daughters
    in Burma,
    and Liberia,
    and East Timor.

Voice 2: And still they cry,
for the children they loved
and lost long since
    in Soweto
    and Sarajevo
    and Belfast.

Voice 3: And still we cry,
for babies who did not live for long,
or never saw the light of day,
or grew up only to be cut down by illness,
abuse, or slaughter.

Leader: A voice was heard in Ramah,
sobbing and loudly lamenting:
it was Rachel weeping for her children,
refusing to be comforted
because they were no more.

(Silence)

A voice is heard in Ramah
and in all the places of sadness.
It is the voice of God,
who as a mother,
has seen the pain of her children
and seen beyond it.

'Keep your voice from weeping
and keep your eyes from tears;
for your grieving has been heard
and your work shall be rewarded.

There is hope for your future.
I have prepared a place for your children
and will keep them in perfect peace,
until the old things have disappeared

and there is a new heaven
and there is a new earth.'

*(Action may follow during instrumental music, a
chant or sung response, then at the conclusion of
the music, all can join the following prayer.)*

Gracious God,
in your motherly heart,
you share and bear the pain
of all who grieve for lost children.

Keep in your kindness
those, whose names are written in our hearts
or on our consciences,
until the day when we see them face to face
and know that our grieving is over
and that all your promises are kept.
AMEN.

The wise man's journey
Epiphany reading 1

Like the other 'Journey' monologues, this should be read directly to the audience or congregation and is best if it is put in a context after the Epiphany reading or before a carol such as AS WITH GLADNESS.

Wise Man: There will be no camels;
we are going on horseback,
at least for some of the way.

And we won't arrive there
a few hours after everyone else.
It will be weeks, perhaps -
or months.

We are not in a hurry.
That is not the way we work;
we are not Europeans.

We will discuss the phenomenon – the star –
and if it does not go away,
and if we still feel curious,
we will travel.

We will look in the wrong place.
Yes I admit that,
because wise men, potentates, intellectuals –
call us what you will –
are not infallible.

We expect a new power
to emerge from the side of the old one.
We expect the destination we seek
to resemble what our common sense deduces.

We will be upset, angry even,
to find that Herod is ignorant
and that his living space is not the birthplace.

We will find it hard
and intellectually demeaning
to bow the knee to the son of refugees.

And all this . . .
all this upset will be compounded
when it comes to journeying back
and we discover
we have to go home by another way.

That is the trouble with God.
He does not let you leave as you came.
He sends you back,
stripped of your presumptions,
making for home by another way.

The gatekeeper
Epiphany script 1

Whoever reads the monologue must sound like a 'bit of a lad'. He is a guard who, in the gatehouse, is talking to a colleague who is about to fall asleep. If the reading is done in full view of the audience or congregation, the Gatekeeper could be seated with a newspaper in front of him. The Narrator's lines may be omitted.

Personnel: **Narrator** *(optional)*
Gatekeeper

Narrator: Jerusalem was the city in which the Royal Palace
and the Temple were located.
It was the place to which foreigners
hoping to see a 'new-born king'
would naturally go.

Gatekeeper: Here, that was a laugh, Marco . . .
These three guys came to the gatehouse
as if they were going to a fancy-dress party.
One starts yapping away thirteen-to-the-dozen.
'Non parlez' . . . says I, in my best Hebrew.

Then another one starts up in our own lingo.
He says they are interested in stars . . .
'Astrology or Astronomy?' . . . says I,
like a cultured intellectual.
'No, just stars,' . . . says they
'in fact, just one star.'

'You've got a lot to choose from
on a night like this,' says I.
Well, you know
what Wednesday night was like, Marco.

Then he changes his tune and starts asking
about a new addition to the royal family.
So I just mentioned briefly

how Herod's wife had died fifteen years ago
and how he, being semi-geriatric,
didn't look much like the father
of a 'little late one'.
Well, they looked quite peeved.
Their eyes went from the sky to the palace to the sky.

So, to save them getting dizzy, I says,
'Well, if it's not the state-house,
maybe you should try the stable.'

And do you know, Marco . . .
are you listening, Marco?
Do you know . . . I think they took me seriously!

# The soldiers
Epiphany script 2

The Christmas story is not a cuddly baby festival. It begins with the fear, based on Old Testament prophecies, of God coming to earth in person. It ends with the threat of a jealous ruler who, though not a Jewish believer, fears that his power might be taken from him.

In this dialogue, two soldiers should stand opposite each other, the one ticking off a list on which are the names of streets which had to be searched for male children. The Narrator's lines may be omitted.

Personnel: **Narrator** (optional)
              Lucius
              Remo

Narrator: Because the Wise Men did not return
                to Herod's palace and inform him
                of Jesus' whereabouts,
                Herod feared for what might happen
                if the 'new born king' survived.

                So, he set into motion a programme of infanticide –
                the systematic slaughter of innocent children,
                all to protect a decadent system.

Lucius: Cromer Street. How many?

Remo: Fourteen, sir.

Lucius: Curran Street?

Remo: Twelve.

Lucius: Derby Lane?

Remo: Seven.

Lucius: Enderby Street?

Remo: Five.

Lucius: Only five?

Remo: Enderby Street was burned down last year, sir.

Lucius: I see . . . Grant Street?

Remo: Eleven.

Lucius: Hope Terrace?

Remo: Fourteen and a girl.

Lucius: Who killed the girl?

Remo: Victor, sir.

Lucius: Did his mother never tell him the difference?
Where were we . . . ?
Hope Terrace . . .
Huntly Street?

Remo: Twelve.

Lucius: Limeburn Street?

Remo: Fourteen.

Lucius: Melville Park?

Remo: Seven.

Lucius: Melville Park Lodge?

Remo: None.

Lucius: There was one in Melville Park Lodge,
according to our information.

Remo: No, sir.
There was one in the barn behind it.

Lucius: Did you get him?

Remo: No, sir,
they had gone the night before.

△ God of God, Light of Light

Epiphany responses

Leader: God of God,
Light of Light,
true God of true God,

ALL: WE BLESS YOU.

Leader: Object of the Magi's search,
subject of an old man's song,
fulfilment of the Baptist's preaching,

ALL: WE BLESS YOU.

Leader: Mary's son,
Joseph's son,
God's only son,

ALL: WE BLESS YOU.

God bless us and disturb us
Epiphany reading 2

The tune, GOD REST YE, MERRY GENTLEMEN, is well known and fits perfectly these words. However, they can be read as a poem equally effectively. The allusions in the last verse may be changed or updated according to circumstances

---

God bless us and disturb us
as we celebrate the feast,
which marks how heaven's highest
came to earth to be the least.
Lest we consign to Satan's power
all those whose joy has ceased;

> O COME, CHRIST THE SAVIOUR
> FROM BELOW, FROM ABOVE
> AND INFECT THE DEPTHS OF EARTH
> WITH HEAVENLY LOVE.

Where single-parent families
cannot cope with Santa Claus;
where patient folk in Ireland
work for peace without applause;
where politicians hide behind
smooth talk and senseless laws;

Where dealers thrive on heroin
while users writhe in pain;
where helpless mothers watch
their children's lives go down the drain;
where hope's a hit, a shot, a score,
and death becomes a gain;

To Bethlehem, to Bosnia,
Whitehall and Possilpark;
to where a star is needed,
since the dark is doubly dark;
to where our lives require the Lord
to set on them his mark;

Sources of suggested chants and sung responses

AND DID IT HAPPEN?/ John L. Bell;
   Innkeepers and light sleepers (Wild Goose Publications, 1992).
AS WITH GLADNESS/ William Chatterton Dix, Conrad Kocher and William
   Henry Monk; various hymnals.
BE STILL AND KNOW/ John L. Bell;
   Enemy of apathy (Wild Goose Publications, 1988),
   God never sleeps (GIA Publications, 1995).
BEFORE THE WORLD BEGAN (I AM FOR YOU)/ John L. Bell & Graham
   Maule; Heaven shall not wait (Wild Goose Publications, 1987).
BLESS THE LORD, MY SOUL/ Taizé Community;
   Songs and prayers from Taizé (Geoffrey Chapman/ Mowbray 1991)'
   Songs of God's people (Oxford University Press, 1988).
CLOTH FOR THE CRADLE/ John L. Bell & Graham Maule;
   Heaven shall not wait (Wild Goose Publications, 1987).
GLORIA/ traditional;
   Come all you people (Wild Goose Publications, 1995).
GLORIA/ John L. Bell (various);
   Come all you people (Wild Goose Publications, 1995).
GOD REST YE MERRY, GENTLEMEN/ English traditional;
   various hymnals.
HARK THE HERALD ANGELS/ William H. Cummings & Felix
   Mendelssohn-Bartholdy; various hymnals.
I WAITED ON THE LORD/ John L. Bell & Graham Maule;
   Heaven shall not wait (Wild Goose Publications, 1987).
IONA GLORIA/traditional;
   Come all you people (Wild Goose Publications, 1995).
KYRIE/ John L. Bell (various);
   Enemy of apathy (Wild Goose Publications, 1988),
   Come all you people (Wild Goose Publications, 1995).
KYRIE/ Dinah Reindorf (from Ghana);
   Many & great - Songs from the world Church Vol. 1 (Wild Goose
   Publications, 1990).
KYRIE/ Russian Orthodox;
   Songs of God's people (Oxford University Press, 1988).
LITTLE JESUS, SWEETLY SLEEP/ Czech traditional, Percy Dearmer;
   The popular carol book (Mowbray, 1991).
MAGNIFICAT/ John L. Bell & Graham Maule;
   Heaven shall not wait (Wild Goose Publications, 1987).
O LORD, HEAR MY PRAYER/ Taizé Community;
   Songs and prayers from Taizé (Geoffrey Chapman/ Mowbray 1991),
   Songs of God's people (Oxford University Press, 1988).
ON GOD ALONE I WAIT SILENTLY/ John L. Bell;
   Psalms of patience, protest & praise (Wild Goose Publications, 1993).
ONCE IN JUDAH'S LEAST KNOWN CITY/ John L. Bell & Graham Maule;
   Heaven shall not wait (Wild Goose Publications, 1987).
THE FIRST NOWELL/ English traditional;
   various hymnals.
VENI IMMANUEL/ John L. Bell;
   Innkeepers and light sleepers (Wild Goose Publications, 1992).

Major Feasts of the Seasons with their themes

SEASON OF ADVENT

First Sunday
The promised coming of the Messiah.
God's waiting people.

Second Sunday
The Word of God in the Old Testament.
The prophets.

Third Sunday
The Imminent Messiah.
The witness of John the Baptist.

Fourth Sunday
God's decision to come to earth.
Mary, mother of Jesus.

8th December
The Immaculate Conception of the Blessed Virgin Mary.

24th December
Christmas Eve.

25th December
Christmas Day.

SEASON OF CHRISTMAS

First Sunday
The Holy Family.

Second Sunday
The Word become flesh.

26th December
The Feast of St. Stephen, the first martyr.

27th December
The Feast of St. John, apostle & evangelist.

28th December
The Feast of Holy Innocents, martyrs.

1st January
New Year's Day.
Solemnity of the Blessed Virgin Mary.

SEASON OF EPIPHANY

6th January
The Epiphany of our Lord.

Readings for the Seasons and Saint's Days

The regular readings are taken from the Three year Lectionary which, for the greater part is shared by Roman Catholic, Anglican and Protestant churches. The readings for Saints days comes from the Roman Missal.

Seasonal lectionary (Advent to Epiphany)

SEASON OF ADVENT

	YEAR A Beginning on the First Sunday of Advent in 1992, 1995, 1998, 2001, 2004, 2007, 2010, 2013, 2016	YEAR B Beginning on the First Sunday of Advent in 1993, 1996, 1999, 2002, 2005, 2008, 2011, 2014, 2017	YEAR C Beginning on the First Sunday of Advent in 1994, 1997, 2000, 2003, 2006, 2009, 2012, 2015, 2018
First Sunday of Advent *between November 27 and December 3*	Isaiah 2 : 1 - 5 Psalm 122 Romans 13 : 11 - 14 Matthew 24 : 36 - 44	Isaiah 64 : 1 - 9 Psalm 80 : 1 - 7, 17 - 19 1 Corinthians 1 : 3 - 9 Mark 13 : 24 - 37	Jeremiah 33 : 14 - 16 Psalm 25 : 1 - 10 1 Thessalonians 3 : 9 - 13 Luke 21 : 25 - 36
Second Sunday of Advent *between December 4 and December 10*	Isaiah 11 : 1 - 10 Psalm 72 : 1 - 7, 18 - 19 Romans 15 : 4 - 13 Matthew 3 : 1 - 12	Isaiah 40 : 1 - 11 Psalm 85 : 1 - 2, 8 - 13 2 Peter 3 : 8 - 15a Mark 1 : 1 - 8	Malachi 3 : 1 - 4 Psalm 27 or Luke 1 : 68 - 79 Philippians 1 : 3 - 11 Luke 3 : 1 - 6
Third Sunday of Advent *between December 11 and December 17*	Isaiah 35 : 1 - 10 Psalm 146 : 5 - 10 or Luke 1 : 47 - 55 James 5 : 7 - 10 Matthew 11 : 2 - 11	Isaiah 61 : 1 - 4, 8 - 11 Psalm 126 or Luke 1 : 47 - 55 1 Thessalonians 5 : 16 - 24 John 1 : 6 - 8, 19 - 28	Zephaniah 3 : 14 - 20 Psalm 45 or Isaiah 12 : 2 - 6 Philippians 4 : 4 - 7 Luke 3 : 7 - 18
Fourth Sunday of Advent *December 18 and December 24*	Isaiah 7 : 10 - 16 Psalm 80 : 1 - 7, 17 - 19 Romans 1 : 1 - 7 Matthew 1 : 18 - 25	2 Samuel 7 : 1 - 11, 16 Psalm 89 : 1 - 4, 19 - 26 or Luke 1 : 47 - 55 Romans 16 : 25 - 27 Luke 1 : 26 - 38	Micah 5 : 2 - 5a Psalm 80 : 1 - 7 or Luke 1 : 47 - 55 Hebrews 10 : 5 - 10 Luke 1 : 39 - 45, (46 - 55)

SEASON OF CHRISTMAS

Nativity of the Lord (Christmas Day)

Any of the three sets of reading may be used on Christmas Eve/Day.

The readings from II and III may be used as alternatives for Christmas Day.

If III is not used on Christmas Day, it should be used at some service during the Christmas cycle because of the significance of the prologue of John's Gospel.

	YEAR A Beginning on the First Sunday of Advent in 1992, 1995, 1998, 2001, 2004, 2007, 2010, 2013, 2016	YEAR B Beginning on the First Sunday of Advent in 1993, 1996, 1999, 2002, 2005, 2008, 2011, 2014, 2017	YEAR C Beginning on the First Sunday of Advent in 1994, 1997, 2000, 2003, 2006, 2009, 2012, 2015, 2018
I			
Isaiah	9 : 2 - 7	9 : 2 - 7	9 : 2 - 7
Psalm	96	96	96
Titus	2 : 11 - 14	2 : 11 - 14	2 : 11 - 14
Luke	2 : 1 -14, (15 -20)	2 : 1 -14, (15 -20)	2 : 1 -14, (15 -20)
II			
Isaiah	62 : 6 - 12	62 : 6 - 12	62 : 6 - 12
Psalm	97	97	97
Titus	3 : 4 - 7	3 : 4 - 7	3 : 4 - 7
Luke	2 :(1 - 7), 8 -20	2 :(1 - 7), 8 -20	2 :(1 - 7), 8 -20
III			
Isaiah	52 : 7 - 10	52 : 7 - 10	52 : 7 - 10
Psalm	98	98	98
Hebrews	1 : 1 - 4, (5 -12)	1 : 1 - 4, (5 -12)	1 : 1 - 4, (5 -12)
John	1 : 1 - 14	1 : 1 - 14	1 : 1 - 14

First Sunday after Christmas

These readings are used on the First Sunday after Christmas unless the readings for the Epiphany of the Lord are preferred.

	YEAR A	YEAR B	YEAR C
	Isaiah 63 : 7 - 9	Isaiah 61 : 10-62 : 3	1 Samuel 2 : 18-20, 26
	Psalm 148	Psalm 148	Psalm 148
	Hebrews 2 : 10 - 18	Galatians 4 : 4 - 7	Colossians 3 : 12 -17
	Matthew 2 : 13 - 23	Luke 2 : 22 - 40	Luke 2 : 41 -52

	YEAR A Beginning on the First Sunday of Advent in 1992, 1995, 1998, 2001, 2004, 2007, 2010, 2013, 2016	**YEAR B** Beginning on the First Sunday of Advent in 1993, 1996, 1999, 2002, 2005, 2008, 2011, 2014, 2017	**YEAR C** Beginning on the First Sunday of Advent in 1994, 1997, 2000, 2003, 2006, 2009, 2012, 2015, 2018
January 1 – **The Naming of Jesus**	Numbers 6 : 22 - 27 Psalm 8 Galatians 4 : 4 - 7 　or Philippians 2 : 5 - 11 Luke 2 : 15 - 21	Numbers 6 : 22 - 27 Psalm 8 Galatians 4 : 4 - 7 　or Philippians 2 : 5 - 11 Luke 2 : 15 - 21	Numbers 6 : 22 - 27 Psalm 8 Galatians 4 : 4 - 7 　or Philippians 2 : 5 - 11 Luke 2 : 15 - 21
January 1 – **when observed as** **New Year's Day**	Ecclesiastes 3 : 1 - 13 Psalm 8 Revelation 21 : 1 - 6a Matthew 25 : 31 - 46	Ecclesiates 3 : 1 - 13 Psalm 8 Revelation 21 : 1 - 6a Matthew 25 : 31 - 46	Ecclesiastes 3 : 1 - 13 Psalm 8 Revelation 21 : 1 - 6a Matthew 25 : 31 - 46
Second Sunday after **Christmas Day** *These readings are provided for* *use when Epiphany (January 6)* *is celebrated on a weekday* *following the Second Sunday* *after Christmas Day.*	Jeremiah 31 : 7 - 14 Psalm 147 : 12 - 20 Ephesians 1 : 3 - 14 John 1 : (1 - 9), 10 - 18	Jeremiah 31 : 7 - 14 Psalm 147 : 12 - 20 Ephesians 1 : 3 - 14 John 1 : (1 - 9), 10 - 18	Jeremiah 31 : 7 - 14 Psalm 147 : 12 - 20 Ephesians 1 : 3 - 14 John 1 : (1 - 9), 10 - 18
SEASON OF EPIPHANY **Epiphany of the Lord**	Isaiah 60 : 1 - 6 Psalm 72 : 1 - 7, 10 - 14 Ephesians 3 : 1 - 12 Matthew 2 : 1 - 12	Isaiah 60 : 1 - 6 Psalm 72 : 1 - 7, 10 - 14 Ephesians 3 : 1 - 12 Matthew 2 : 1 - 12	Isaiah 60 : 1 - 6 Psalm 72 : 1 - 7, 10 - 14 Ephesians 3 : 1 - 12 Matthew 2 : 1 - 12

Proper of Saints (Advent to Epiphany)

8th December
The Immaculate Conception
of the Blessed Virgin Mary.

Genesis	3	:	9 - 15, 20
Psalm	97	:	1 - 4
Ephesians	1	:	3 - 6, 11 - 12
St. Luke	1	:	26 - 38

26th December
St. Stephen, First Martyr

Acts	6	:	8 - 10
	7	:	54 - 59
Psalm	30	:	3 - 4, 6, 8, 16 - 17
St. Matthew	10	:	17 - 22

27th December
St. John, Apostle & Evangelist

St John	1	:	1 - 4
Psalm	96	:	1 - 2, 5 - 6, 11 - 12
John	20	:	2 - 8

28th December
The Holy Innocents, Martyrs

St John	1	:	5 - 2 : 2
Psalm	123	:	2 - 5, 7 - 8
St Matthew	2	:	13 - 18

1st January
Solemnity of Mary, Mother of God.
(readings as for Naming of Jesus)

Index of first lines

The character or speaker is indicated after each first line. For scripts or readings where the first line is that of the Narrator (and which may, in any case, be optional), the first line of the next character or speaker is also given.

The Wild Goose Resource & Worship Groups

The **Wild Goose Resource Group** is an expression of the Iona Community's commitment to the renewal of public worship. Based in Glasgow, the Group has four members (Alison Adam, John Bell, Graham Maule and Mairi Munro) who are employed full-time and who lead workshops and seminars throughout Britain and abroad.

The WGRG's sister Group, the **Wild Goose Worship Group** (to which the four WGRG workers also belong) consists of sixteen members, who represent a variety of occupations and denominations.

Both Groups are engaged in developing and identifying new methods and materials to enable the revitalisation of congregational song, prayer and worship. Their songs and liturgical material are frequently broadcast on radio and television.

The WGRG publishes a twice-yearly newsletter, **Goose*Gander*,** to enable friends and supporters to keep abreast of WGWG and WGRG developments. If you would like to receive Goose*Gander,* please copy and complete the form overleaf.

Wild Goose Resource & Worship Groups
Mailing list
CFTC

Yes, I would like to receive **Goose*Gander.***

NAME ....

ADDRESS ....

....

POSTCODE..**DATE** ....

I'd also like to receive further information regarding:

☐ **Mail Order Catalogue**

☐ **The Iona Community**

☐ **Ways to support the WGRG**

Please return to:
WILD GOOSE RESOURCE GROUP,
Iona Community, Pearce Institute,
840 Govan Road,
Glasgow G51 3UU, Scotland
(0141-445-4561 ext.30)

The Iona Community

The Iona Community is an ecumenical Christian community, founded in 1938 by the Late Lord MacLeod of Fuinary (the Revd George MacLeod DD) and committed to seeking new ways of living the Gospel in today's world. Gathered around the rebuilding of the ancient monastic buildings of Iona Abbey, but with its original inspiration in the poorest areas of Glasgow during the Depression, the Community has sought ever since the 'rebuilding of the common life', bringing together work and worship, prayer and politics, the sacred and the secular in ways that reflect its strongly incarnational theology.

The Community today is a movement of some 200 Members, over 1,400 Associate Members and about 1,600 Friends. The Members – women and men from many backgrounds and denominations, most in Britain, but some overseas – are committed to a rule of daily prayer and Bible reading, sharing and accounting for their use of time and money, regular meeting and action for justice and peace.

The Iona Community maintains three centres on Iona and Mull: Iona Abbey and the MacLeod Centre on Iona, and Camas Adventure Camp on the Ross of Mull. Its base is in Community House, Glasgow, where it also supports work with young people, the Wild Goose Resource and Worship Groups, a bimonthly magazine (Coracle) and a publishing house (Wild Goose Publications).

For further information on the Iona Community please contact:

The Iona Community,
Pearce Institute,
840 Govan Road,
Glasgow
G51 3UU

Tel. 0141 445 4561; Fax. 0141 445 4295
e-mail: ionacomm@gla.iona.org.uk
http://www.iona.org.uk